THE WINE SNOB'S DICTIONARY

Also by David Kamp

The Film Snob's Dictionary—with Lawrence Levi

The Rock Snob's Dictionary—with Steven Daly

The Food Snob's Dictionary—with Marion Rosenfeld

THE WINE SNOB'S DICTIONARY

AN ESSENTIAL LEXICON OF
OENOLOGICAL KNOWLEDGE

Wine Snob *n*: reference term for the sort of wine
obsessive for whom the actual joy of drinking wine
is but a sideline to the accumulation of
arcane knowledge about it

David Kamp
and David Lynch

Illustrated by Ross MacDonald

BROADWAY BOOKS   NEW YORK

PUBLISHED BY BROADWAY BOOKS

Copyright © 2008 by David Kamp

All Rights Reserved

Published in the United States by Broadway Books, an imprint of
The Doubleday Publishing Group,
a division of Random House, Inc., New York.
www.broadwaybooks.com

Portions of the material published herein previously appeared in *Vanity Fair*.

BROADWAY BOOKS and its logo, a letter B bisected on the diagonal,
are trademarks of Random House, Inc.

Book design by Ellen Cipriano

Library of Congress Cataloging-in-Publication Data
Kamp, David.
The Wine snob's dictionary : an essential lexicon of oenological knowledge /
David Kamp and David Lynch ; illustrated by Ross MacDonald.
p. cm.
1. Wine and wine making—Dictionaries. I. Lynch, David. II. Title
TP546.K36 2008
641.2'203—dc22
2008004480

ISBN 978-0-7679-2692-8

PRINTED IN THE UNITED STATES OF AMERICA

5 7 9 10 8 6 4

Contents

Acknowledgments

The authors wish to thank Aimée Bell, Josie Peltz, Graydon Carter, James F. Bell III, Dana Brown, Rob Allen, Melissa Davis, Andrus and Andrew Gates, Peter Richmond, Steve Rubin, Charles Conrad, Jenna Thompson, Suzanne Gluck, Georgia Cool, Sarah Ceglarski, and the late Art Cooper. And the good earth and its indisputable sense of *terroir*. And the bibulous but unbelligerent people with expense accounts.

An Introductory Note
by the Authors

Wine Snob. Isn't that a redundancy, like saying *wet rain* or *nuisance telemarketer?*

Well, yes—there's no getting around it. Central to the very premise of wine appreciation is the notion that it requires an advanced skill set; that, in order to most fully understand and enjoy the experience of sniffing and sipping fermented grape juice, one must have a cache of special knowledge *to which mere ordinary people do not have access.*

Wine Snobbery is, therefore, the default state of the wine enthusiast. In this regard, it is unique among Cultural Snobberies. In other realms, such as music, film, and food, the Snobs are the hard cases, the ones who have taken their passions to irrational extremes—devoting their lives to, say, the post-Monkees work of Michael Nesmith, or frame-by-frame dissections of Peter Jackson's early splatter pics, or the pursuit of the perfect round of Portuguese semisoft sheep's-milk cheese made with thistle rennet. We recognize such figures as grotesques, at best euphemizing them as "intense," at worst calling them out as scary nutjobs.*

The Wine Snob, on the other hand, can sit judgmentally as a bottle is presented to him, watch intently as its contents are decanted and poured, swirl the liquid centrifugally in his glass, hold the glass up to the light, lower it under his nose, close his eyes, take a sip, pause in contemplation, open his eyes, and declare what he has just drunk to be "Complex, cola and pencil-lead on the nose, with leather, dust, barnyard, and raspberry on the mid-palate, and a medium-long, tannic finish"—and not only will this man *not* be led away in restraints to the sanitorium, he will find himself actually being admired for his taste and acumen.

Far from existing on the freaky margins of society, like the ever-resentful Rock Snob or the madly dogmatic Food Snob, the Wine Snob commands center stage in his chosen area of cultural fanaticism. So why, then, should a book such as this one exist? Aren't there already plenty of wine references out there that are de facto guides to Wine Snobbery? In a world where li-

---

*For more information on Rock Snobs, Film Snobs, and Food Snobs, see, respectively, *The Rock Snob's Dictionary,* by David Kamp and Steven Daly (Broadway Books, 2005); *The Film Snob's Dictionary,* by David Kamp with Lawrence Levi (Broadway Books, 2006); and *The Food Snob's Dictionary,* by David Kamp and Marion Rosenfeld (Broadway Books, 2007).

brary shelves groan with multiple titles by the likes of Jancis Robinson, Oz Clarke, Hugh Johnson, and Andrea Robinson, is a *Wine Snob's Dictionary* really necessary?

Why This Book Is Really Necessary

As much as the Wine Snob is widely and correctly perceived to be the archetypal wine connoisseur, his profile and tendencies—precisely who he is—are only dimly understood. There persists an outmoded notion that the Wine Snob is necessarily wealthy, wellborn, and Francophilic, when, in fact, Wine Snobbery has many faces, some of them surprisingly homely. Indeed, one of the reasons the 2004 film *Sideways* proved so jarring was that it revealed a breed of Wine Snob that, while eminently recognizable to other Snobs, was unfamiliar to the public: a drab schlub who knows his stuff and commands the respect of winemakers and pourers, but who is also professionally unsuccessful and abjectly unglamorous. (Indeed, the film's surprise-hit status sent Snobs into defense mode, railing against purported slights and inaccuracies: *C'mon, the Central Coast isn't even representative of the rest of California! He's* totally wrong *about Merlot— it only happens to underpin some of the greatest Bordeaux of all time! Well, let me tell you that* I've *never stolen money from my mother!*)

There are Wine Snobs all around us, and they range widely in age, income bracket, and hair length. There's the standard-issue hedonist-aesthete, for whom Wine Snobbery is another trait in the portfolio, along with the vintage-car fetish and the permanent tan. There's the hippie-ish evangelist who wears muddied boots and baggy shorts, and likes to remind you that viticulture is a kind of *farming,* man, and that the juice you're diggin' tells a magical story about the special chunk of earth from which its grapes came. There's the NFL offensive lineman who's spent his signing bonus on an insta-cellar and learned about wine from the top down, evolving from label whore ("Pétrus! *Awesome!*") into shrewd collector ("An Araujo vertical! *Awesome!*").

Put simply, you never know when or where you're going to encounter a Wine Snob. And then, before you know it, you're weathering a storm of terms like *malo, extracted,* and *Cab Franc leafiness* that leaves you feeling bewildered, humiliated, and inclined to drink nothing but beer (which will expose you to Microbrew Snobs, who speak a still-more-incomprehensible language of "porters," "doppelbocks," and "dunkel weiss," but never mind).

The Wine Snob's Dictionary equips its reader with the tools and survival skills to endure a Wine Snob encounter, and possibly even disarm the Snob with a casual reference that he doesn't see coming—to, say, "the '78 La Tâche I was fortunate enough to share with

Aubert," or "the damnable, spoofalated swill that the McMansioners drink." The book further serves as a helpful cheat sheet for those who simply wish to understand advanced-placement wine chat without actually getting caught up in tastings and spit buckets, and as a legitimate study guide for trainee Snobs who aspire to be wine professionals. Would-be sommeliers are warned, however, that even a book such as this is no substitute for experience, runty stature, a persecution complex, and a tightly cinched dark suit offset by an assaultively loud necktie.

A Brief History of Wine Snobbery

Though references to wine abound in the Bible and in ancient classical literature (the word *symposium* is a corruption of a Greek term meaning "drinking party"), Wine Snobbery as we know it dates back only to the middle of the nineteenth century. It was in 1855, on the occasion of that year's Exposition Universelle de Paris, that Napoléon III enlisted his country's wine merchants to put together a system of ranking and categorization for its finest Bordeaux wines. The result, the Bordeaux Wine Official Classification of 1855—or, in Snob shorthand, the 1855 CLASSIFICATION (see entry, page 25)—was at once baldly hierarchical and utterly idiosyncratic: ideal breeding conditions for Snobbery.

There were already plenty of wineshops in the Anglophone world—such as London's Berry Bros. & Rudd, founded in 1698, and New York's Acker, Merrall & Condit, founded in 1820—but the advent of a classification system, with its *Premier Crus* (first growths) and exalted châteaux, equipped wine-lovers with a common set of standards to be upheld, absorbed, dissected, and showboated. In Britain especially, it became the mark of a true oenophile to drink one's way through all the classified Bordeaux and jot down TASTING NOTES (see entry, page 92) about one's impressions, as much for purposes of social one-upmanship as for one's own edification.

The image of the Wine Snob as a fancy English or Anglophile toff remains powerful in the public imagination, as antiquated as it now is; only the white-haired wine sage MICHAEL BROADBENT (see entry, page 10) has legitimately played such a role in contemporary Snob discourse. But not for nothing has the image persisted in America. The period of Prohibition, from 1920 to 1933, was such a profound setback to winemaking in the United States that it really wasn't until the 1970s that there was enough indigenous wine of high quality to get Snobby about. Prior to the Nixon presidency, American Wine Snobs, their ranks thin and suspiciously émigré-heavy, looked invariably to Europe.

But in the '70s, events conspired to legitimize

both American wine and American oenophilia, opening entirely new frontiers for Wine Snobbery. In the so-called JUDGMENT OF PARIS (see entry, page 52), a collection of condescending French judges, presumably on loan from central casting, convened for a blind tasting of French and American wines, and, to their utter consternation, reserved their highest praise for a Chardonnay crafted by Napa Valley winemaker Mike Grgich and a Cabernet Sauvignon crafted by Napa Valley winemaker WARREN WINIARSKI (see entry, page 110). Near the end of the decade, a thirtysomething Maryland lawyer named ROBERT PARKER (see entry, page 69) gave flight to his latent Wine Snob urges and came out with a newsletter called the *Baltimore-Washington Wine Advocate* (its name later shortened) that connected with a like-minded audience of young adults who pleasured in tilting balloon glasses into their faces for extended periods of time.

Parker instituted a practice of rating wines on a 100-point scale, which, while more user-friendly and easier to comprehend than the Bordeaux classifications, essentially opened up *all* wines to scrutiny and discussion. Suddenly, there was much more wine out there to be knowing about, and much more knowingness to be achieved through borrowed opinion. The *Wine Advocate* became, and remains, a Snob juggernaut.

As is so often the case in Snob discourse, where yesterday's indie band/film/coffeehouse becomes today's corporate sellout, the upstart Parker soon enough morphed into the Establishment, bemoaned for his outsize influence and alleged preference for "international-style" wines whose makers have crafted their products just to please him. Yet this has hardly sounded the death knell for Wine Snobbery; rather, it has created a powerful new strain of Reverse Snobbery in which wines and winemakers are esteemed for existing off the Parker grid. As with Food Snobbery, which has taken on a locavorist, sustainable-ista, sociopolitical dimension in recent years, Wine Snobbery is now sometimes informed by a crunchy consciousness that finds its adherents proclaiming their fealty to the purity of *TERROIR* (see entry, page 93) and ZERO-MANIPULATION wines (see entry, page 111).

Meanwhile, Parker's Establishment Snobbery trundles ever onward, turning small-batch favorites like Screaming Eagle Cabernet Sauvingnon and Mollydooker Velvet Glove Shiraz into feverishly pursued CULT WINES (see entry, page 18). And somewhere, heard faintly from old drawing rooms with faded wallpaper and Noël Coward playing on the Victrola, there still persist a few members of the old Brit-Snob school who insist on calling an aroma a "bouquet" and a red Bordeaux a CLARET (see entry, page 13). Wine Snobbery is, like the wines it inordinately celebrates, a living thing that changes over time.*

Helpful Hints

Given the complexities and interconnections of the Snob universe, cross-references between entries are common and are spelled out in CAPITAL LETTERS for easy identification. The editors have also seen fit to identify certain entries with ⧠, the Wine Snob Vanguard icon, which depicts the black or shaded blind-tasting glass used by experts and sommeliers when stunt-tasting for public approbation. The blind-tasting glass keeps out light and lends no visual clue to what its contents might be. And yet it's said that the dean of American sommeliers, LARRY STONE (see entry, page 86), is capable, on days when his palate has brought its A-game to a blind tasting, to divine not only the vintage and grape variety of what he's sampled, but the specific producer. It is only fitting, then, that the presence of the blind-tasting glass icon

---

*Indeed, readers who feel that this slender volume has not adequately addressed the latest in Snob trends and fetishes are welcome to visit www.snobsite.com to aggravate the authors with complaints and purported glaring omissions. The authors reserve the right to use said Web site to pass their own judgment on developing Wine Snob trends, and also to reciprocate abuse from readers.

should indicate, in this book, an entry that is held in especially high regard by Wine Snobs—for example, the intimidatingly esteemed Burgundy estate Domaine de la Romanée-Conti (or DRC for short; see entry, page 23), or the GRAND AWARD (see entry, page 34), the prestigious distinction bestowed by the *Wine Spectator* upon the Snobworthiest, most extensive wine lists in the world.

Finally, let us express our sincere hope that the knowledge collected herein serves you well on the path to Snob enlightenment and to a more mannered, ridiculous approach to wine-drinking. And if that doesn't work, at least this book makes a good coaster.

THE WINE SNOB'S
DICTIONARY

The Wine Snob's
Dictionary

A 🍷 symbol indicates a Wine Snob Vanguard item,
denoting a person, an entity, or a concept held in
particular esteem by Wine Snobs.

Aaron, Sam. Revered New York wine merchant
(1912–1996) who was the chief evangelist behind
Sherry-Lehmann Wine and Spirits, the landmark
Upper East Side shop owned by his family. In partner-
ship with his older brother Jack, who purchased
the shop shortly after the repeal of Prohibition, Sam,
a trained psychologist and protégé of FRANK
SCHOONMAKER, shepherded in the era of upper-
middle-class American wine connoisseurship, writing
florid, proto–J. Petermanesque copy for Sherry-
Lehmann's catalog and enlisting American-food guru
James Beard as a fellow copywriter and sometime in-
store greeter. *If it weren't for ol' Sam Aaron, bless him,*

we'd all still be drinking rum toddies and backyard moonshine.

Acidity. Crucial, fairly self-explanatory component of STRUCTURE in wine; the cause of the palate-puckering tartness that either excites or repels the Snob taster, depending on whether said Snob is a devotee of more measured, traditional wine styles or a hedonistic guzzler of FRUIT BOMBS.

Aerator. Unnecessary status gadget, often fashioned of crystal, that hastens the process of getting a wine to "open up," obviating the arriviste Snob's need for patience or traditional decanting. Most aerators require the user to awkwardly and cumbersomely hold them over a glass while wine is poured through them. Many aerators pass themselves off as objets d'art to justify their steep prices, though they generally resemble the sort of whimsical "folk art" sold by rich men's wives in resort-town gift shops.

Ah So. Generic term for a two-pronged wine-bottle opener that, given that it isn't technically a screw-pull device, is better described as a "cork extractor" than a corkscrew. The Ah So's user slips one prong between the cork and the bottle, and then the other, rocking the opener back and forth until it shimmies down the length of the cork.

Ah So

Classicist Snobs prefer the Ah So to such devices as Metrokane's chic, expensive Rabbit corkscrew because it grips the cork from its sides rather than the middle, an especially valuable trait with old, wet, quick-to-crumble stoppers that cling stubbornly to the interiors of aged trophy bottles.

Appellation d'Origine Controllée (**AOC**). Strict, government-regulated classification system used in France since the 1930s to delimit the geographical origins of the country's more prestigious wines (as well as certain Franco-exalted foods, such as cheese). Despite the phrase's literal translation as "controlled appellation," the rules determining which wines qualify for AOC status have been assembled with all the clarity and consistency of tax code—a circumstance exploited by Snobs and Frenchmen, who count on the system's impenetrability to retain mystique and keep novitiates out of the Snob club. AOC appellations extend beyond mere geography, functioning as prescriptions for all facets of production: the types of grapes used, the allowable grape yields, and even winemaking and aging techniques.

Asher, Gerald. Authentically writerly wine writer, British-born but spiritually and physically based in the Bay Area, where, like ROBERT FINIGAN, he served as a firsthand witness to the Napa-Sonoma grapequake. A refugee from the midcentury London wine trade, where he bucked BROADBENT-ian mores by focusing on France's less hoity-toity, better-value wines, Asher found himself Stateside in the early 1970s and found his métier as the wine sage of *Gourmet*, a role he holds to this day.

Attack. Martial term deployed by machismo-minded Snobs to describe the first impression a wine makes as it storms the sensory beach that is one's palate. Used especially in reference to the sweetness that is naturally picked up by receptors on the tip of the tongue. *The* attack *on the '99 Chambolle was an intense blast of ripe, round, red fruit, followed by a generously proportioned mid-palate and a long, lingering finish of East Asian spices and beechwood smoke.*

Balance. The quality achieved in a wine when its fruit, ACIDITY, alcohol, and TANNIN are all in good proportion to one another. While a reasonably straightforward term, especially by wine-talk standards, *balance* nonetheless sounds obtuse or off to the non-Snob ear, somehow evoking strange images of balloon glasses fitted with calipers.

Barnyard. Counterintuitively positive adjective for wines with a pronounced earthiness; the Wine Snob analog to the Food Snob term *lusty. There's a healthy dose of* barnyard *funk on the nose of this Echézeaux.*

Barrel tasting. Literally, a sampling of a wine drawn directly from the barrel in which it is aging; socially, a means by which wine critics and other professionals may flaunt their access and avidity. While it is common for the winemaker himself to sneak a peek of a wine as it matures in its oak vessel, the better to keep tabs on its evolution and quality, it's a more rarified occasion for the non-winemaker, who prizes the experience as much for its me-firstness as for the insight it provides. *The 2005, which I had occasion to try at a* barrel tasting *with Jean-Michel this past spring, prom-*

ises to be one of the greatest releases of the last twenty-five years from this fabled château.

Barrique. A 225-liter oak barrel used to age wine. In the olden days of winemaking, a wood barrel was simply a vessel in which to transport wine, but after it was realized that oak imparts pleasing flavors and textures to wine, *barriques*—especially new ones custom-built from French oak—became the ultimate symbol of vintnerific sophistication. Depending on a Snob's persuasion, *barrique* aging is either a glorious source of oak-derived notes of vanilla, *PAIN GRILLÉ,* and tof-

fee (progressive modernist with a second home in Sonoma) or a vile abomination (aging classicist who publishes his own newsletter).

Barrique

Bead. Winespeak term for the bubbles in a glass of Champagne, which are purported to string together into a beadlike formation—ideally, a formation that is daintily delicate (the smaller the bubbles, the better) and persistent (the bubbles should still be snaking upward as you take your last sip). *The mature, straw-gold color of the '95 Krug was accentuated by a lovely, finely woven* bead *and a nose of baker's yeast and Seckel pears.*

Betts, Richard. Dreamy, swishy-haired, new-paradigm MASTER SOMMELIER who serves as the wine director at the Little Nell, a swank Aspen inn and resort. The antithesis of the imperious, TASTEVIN-wearing sommelier of yore, Betts, a mountain biker and trained geologist, exudes a hempy, Perry Farrell–ish looseness and cultivates envy among year-round restaurant floor-patrollers by not only overseeing a GRAND AWARD–winning list but also enjoying a six-month-long off-season during which he makes private-label wines in France, Australia, and elsewhere.

Richard Betts

Biodynamics. Intense, holier-than-organic farming movement inspired by the lectures given in the early twentieth century by the philosopher and education innovator Rudolf Steiner (1861–1925). The ethos of choice for Wine Snobs who think that even the organic movement has gone too corporate, Biodynamics is based on the concept of the farm as a self-sufficient, mixed-use organism dependent on the interrelatons of the realms animal, mineral, vegetable, and, indeed, *cosmological.* (Adherents believe that interplanetary relations play a role in healthy plant growth.) Though the French dominate *biodynamie* discourse as it relates to wine, thanks to such noisy testifiers as Nicolas Joly in the Loire Valley and Chapoutier in the Rhône, the movement is increasingly embraced by progressivists and infrequent bathers the world over.

Bohr, Robert. Wunderkind member of the celebrity-sommelier constellation who established himself at Cru, a New York City restaurant that became an instant Snob mecca when it opened in 2004. A Francocentrist despite his New Jersey roots and English-yobbo appearance, Bohr has adeptly cultivated wealthy collectors and assembled a wine list of such breadth that it takes up two massive leather-bound volumes. Known in Snob circles for his fetish for trophy wines in large-format bottles, which he conspicuously totes around at industry events, dispensing pours to colleagues he deems worthy.

Botrytis cinerea. Pesky fungus that arises in wet, humid conditions, destroying wine grapes or, in controlled circumstances, concentrating their sugar by sapping them of water. In this latter scenario, *Botrytis* infection is known as "noble rot," a phrase trotted out by plummy connoisseurs of expensive dessert wines like Sauternes and TBA (Trockenbeerenauslese). Still, *Botrytis* blight is generally a nuisance to most winemakers and is even the cause of a rare respiratory ailment known as winegrower's lung.

Breed. Supremacist-redolent term used in describing a wine of obviously ritzy pedigree—a wine whose luxurious, refined personality indicates to its knowing appraiser that it is the product of an aristocratic vineyard site, such as a Grand CRU in Burgundy or a First Growth in Bordeaux. *The finely grained tannins, the deep core of cassis fruit, and the exceptionally long and perfumed finish all mark this effort as a wine of great* breed.

Brett. Abbreviation for *Brettanomyces,* a strain of yeast that, when present in wine, causes the wine to smell metallic and taste a bit "off"; usually indicative of less-than-ideal sanitary conditions in a winery. Though professional winemakers are the ones most likely to notice and correctly identify brett, the term is increasingly heard issuing forth from the mouths of sommeliers at industry tastings, often as they attempt to throw competitors and prosperous civilian inter-lopers off guard. *Eiuww, I'm getting a little* brett *on this Cab.*

Brick. Visual descriptor associated with older red wines, which lose color intensity as they age. A wine's passage from RUBY to brick is usually brought about by slow, controlled oxidation over time and is oft the subject of lyrical commentary by Snobs, akin in their minds to a faithful dog's passage from vigorous stick-chaser to gray-muzzled layabout. Less lyrical, how-ever, are those occasions when a *young* wine comes off as brickish, in which case the consternated Snob com-plains that he has some defective JUICE on his hands.

Broadbent, Michael. Droll, prolific, trilby-wearing British wine writer of John Gielgud–ish mien and imposing stature, having long served as the head of the wine department at Christie's and having written the most authoritative books on vintage wines. Adored by Snobs for the voluminous handwritten notes he has kept in red, schoolboy-style exercise

books since the 1950s and for his utter lack of concession to the mores of the ROBERT PARKER era—in a typically Broadbentian utterance, he has decreed that today's "supermarket wines . . . are for drinking, not for writing about."

Michael Broadbent

Burghound. Quarterly newsletter and, in recent years, corresponding Web site run by autodidact wine enthusiast Allen Meadows—like ROBERT PARKER, a refugee from the white-collar ranks (Meadows was the CFO for Fidelity National) who turned his hobby into an enterprise. Focusing exclusively on Burgundy, whose unpredictable wines have historically attracted the most obsessive and masochistic of Wine Snobs, Meadows is respected even by know-it-all Snobs for his ability to parse the region's hopelessly complex network of small producers and tiny vineyards. *Buy up all the '05 you can now; it's been tipped as the best vintage ever by Mr.* Burghound *himself.*

Cap. The crust of grape skins and other solids that forms atop a vat of fermenting red wine. Cap-related ministrations inordinately excite the wonkiest of Wine Snobs, who are familiar with the complementary processes of "punching down" (pushing the cap back down into the liquids to impart color, flavor, and TANNIN) and "pumping over" (pumping juice from the bottom of the tank and spraying it on top of the cap).

Cassis. French word for "black currant" and the liqueur made from same, employed in TASTING NOTES and reviews as the go-to sensual identifier for Cabernet Sauvignon. More experienced Snobs, having mastered this term, then graduate to such advanced Cab descriptors as "bilberry" and "mace." *The '82 Mouton is still showing beautifully, its saturated ruby color still intact along with its dense, youthful flavors of* cassis *and chocolate.*

Cellar management. Newfangled "service" marketed to serious collectors, in which a wine merchant or expert oversees the assembly and maintenance of a client's cellar: ensuring that certain wines are stashed away for aging, that bottles are properly tagged, that the storage conditions are good, that the collection is sufficiently balanced between wine regions and types, etc. A uniquely first-world and unnecessary result of dot-com and hedge-fund wealth. *Our trained and well-traveled team offers a varied portfolio of* cellar management *solutions.*

Château Cheval Blanc. Bordeaux estate in Saint-Émilion whose wines are a slightly offbeat target of Snob adulation—the Thelonious Monk to Château Margaux's Miles Davis. Lush and generous when young, Cheval Blanc, which has an unusually high percentage of the Cabernet Franc grape in its blend, has a fervent cult whose members consider its 1947 vintage to be the greatest wine ever made. *My most recent tasting of the '47* Cheval Blanc *showed it to be very much alive, almost portlike in its intensity.*

Chewy. Ordinary adjective put to hyperbolic use when applied to wine, suggesting that the JUICE in question is so dense that it requires actual mastication. *The big,* chewy *tannins on this Zin have got me jonesin' for a steak!*

Cigar box. Improbable Snob tasting term, commonly applied to deep, dark reds of the Cabernet family— Franc especially, but also Sauvignon. *Lovely aromas of black currant and* cigar box *carry through to the long and harmonious finish.*

Claret. Quaint term for a red Bordeaux, still used in England (especially by MICHAEL BROADBENT) and revived in recent years by such American producers as Francis Coppola and Su Hua Newton, who trot out "claret" even though their wines aren't from Bordeaux.

Clarke, Oz. Bald, English, Oxford-educated, relentlessly chipper pocket-guide specialist who took up wine-writing as a second career after his West End acting career got stuck in idle. While not taken terribly seriously by Snobs, given his multimedia ubiquity and penchant for writing portable, softcover books, Clarke was prescient in recognizing the potential of Australian wines, so much so that many novice Snobs labor under the misimpression that he is, in fact, from OZ.

Clendenen, Jim. Falstaffian California winemaker whose Robert Plant mane, floral-print shirts, and dude-ular bonhomie have established him as the face of the laid-back, communal Central Coast, the region affectionately portrayed in *Sideways*. In addition to running the winery Au Bon Climat, Clendenen is also a well-traveled seeker with several Burgundy quests under his belt (Burgundy being the favored destination for spiritual Wine Snob questers;

Jim Clendenen

see also *BURGHOUND*), and his Burgophilia shows in his wines, which incite Paul Giamatti–worthy soliloquies from critics.

Climat. Wine-talk diminutive of *TERROIR,* used to denote the siting of a particular vineyard. Similar in meaning to CRU, but considerably more precious in conversation. *To my mind, no other* climat *delivers wines with the velvety textures of Richebourg.*

Closed. Utiliarian descriptor for any wine that doesn't seem to be giving all of itself, with no immediate suggestions of lychees, huckleberries, or what have you. In younger wines, a synonym, more or less, for TIGHT; in older wines, a sadder, more resigned term, denoting a wine that will never realize greatness, its fruit and aromatics smothered by a tannic towel.

Cocks and Féret. Titter-inducing shorthand for the so-called Bordeaux Bible, *Bordeaux and Its Wines,* a reference book whose first edition was published in France in 1850 (as *Bordeaux et ses vins, Classés par ordre de merité*) by an Englishman, Charles Cocks, and a Frenchman, Michel Féret. Historically significant as the template for the 1855 CLASSIFICATION, upon which Bordeaux classifications are still based, "Cocks and Féret" is

Cocks & Feret

linguistically significant for sounding like an especially filthy piece of Cockney rhyming slang.

Colgin, Ann. Texas-born socialite and former art and antiques dealer whose Colgin Cellars Cabernets, produced in Napa Valley, epitomize CULT WINE fanaticism at its most acute. Since 1992, Colgin has produced hobby-size quantities of wine that have sent the likes of ROBERT PARKER into rapture, prompting lunatic bidding wars at auction and desperate attempts by status seekers to get on her (closed) mailing list. The only way a civilian can sample a Colgin Cellars wine is to pay in the mid-to-upper three figures at a handful of expense-account restaurants—a grave affront to Wine Snobbery's socialist wing, which might also have a problem with Colgin's dog being named Corton-Charlemagne.

Complexity. Elemental Snob vocab-builder, used as an all-purpose compliment to wines for their diversity of flavors, aromas, and textures. Using this term at tastings is an effective if vague way to communicate one's sensual acuity.

Compost tea. Next-gen organic potion upheld by progressive winemakers as the future of viticulture. Made by adding water to compost, letting the mixture steep and ferment, and then straining out the liquid, the "tea" is sprayed on vines or poured into their soil. Theoretically, a well-made compost tea, which can use anything from molasses to fish scraps as a food source for beneficial microorganisms, works as both protection against plant pathogens (such as *BOTRYTIS CINEREA*) and as an enhancer of fruit COMPLEXITY. *I thought we were screwed when we had that wet spring, but damned if that* compost tea *didn't keep the powdery mildew off our Chard grapes.*

Concentrated. Fancy oenological synonym for *rich.* In scientific terms, a wine's concentration is its ratio of grape solids to water; thus, to praise a wine as concentrated is to celebrate its palate-coating viscosity. *The deep ruby color is a tip-off to how marvelously* concentrated *this wine is.*

Côte d'Or. French term, literally meaning "golden slope," that refers to the sweet spot of the Burgundy wine zone, the fertile sliver of land that includes the Côte de Nuits to the north (where most of the Pinot Noir is) and the Côte de Beaune to the south (Chardonnay country). While the Classicist Snob regards the Côte d'Or as the indisputable nexus of fine wine forevermore, the Progressivist Snob masks his inability to afford Côte d'Ors by touting the bona fides of the "lesser" Burgundian regions Chablis, Côte Chalonnaise, Mâconnais, and Beaujolais.

Critter wine. Derisive designation for a mass-market-friendly wine bearing a cute, animal-related name—the foremost example being the ubiquitous Yellow Tail brand of Australian cheapo wines, featuring a kangaroo on the label. Though critter wines matter little in Snob circles, the boffo sales of bottles featuring dogs, cats, waterfowl, and even emus on their labels has prompted some high-end winemakers to capitalize on the craze. Oregon's Owen Roe, for example, has slapped a drawing of an Irish wolfhound on the label of its "value" line, but preserves its Snob cred by calling the line itself O'Reilly's rather than, say, Arfy's Choice or Pinot Snookums.

Cru. French word that literally translates as "growth" (from *croître,* "to grow") but in wine terms denotes a distinguished French vineyard—though less in the prosaic, plot-of-land sense than in that of an enchanted locale where geological, climatological, and *TERROIR*-ological faeries join forces in the name of viticulture. Usually the word is part of some aristocratic classification, e.g., *Grand Cru* ("great growth," which denotes the top of the line in Burgundy) or *cru classé* ("classed growth," which indicates a high-end Bordeaux). Also a popular name for NEW WORLD restaurants and wine bars angling for Euro-mystique and a nose-in-glass crowd. *This breathtaking wine has the opulence and explosiveness so typical of the Musigny* cru.

Cult wine. A wine that is produced in small quantities and commands an inflated price, therefore inspiring irrational demand and Salem-style mass hysteria. Most characteristically a boutique Cabernet from Napa sold only through a mailing list.

THE TEN MOST
PRECIOUSLY
NAMED WINES

Back in 1985, it was refreshing when the
iconoclastic Santa Cruz winemaker Randall
Grahm, of the Bonny Doon Vineyard, forsook
the European tradition of naming wines after
geographic appellations, instead giving one of
his Rhône-style wines the irreverent name Le
Cigare Volant ("the flying cigar," or UFO)—a
reference to the ordinance passed by the
southern Rhône town of Châteauneuf-du-Pape
forbidding UFOs from landing within the
town's limits. While Grahm gets a pass from
Wine Snobs because of his likability and the
overall quality of his lineup, he still has a lot to
answer for: a New World epidemic of precious
and cringeworthy wine names and labels that
has now spread to the Old World, where a

Languedoc Chardonnay called Fat Bastard has become an international bestseller.

1. Merlot Over and Play Dead. Standard-bearer for the unfortunate "critter brand" explosion, from the aggressively cute Mutt Lynch Winery in Sonoma's Dry Creek.

2. Chateau La Paws Côte du Boan Roan. More doggy whimsy and pan-linguistic punning, this time, tragically, from California-Zin powerhouse Rosenblum Cellars, which ought to know better.

3. Goats do Roam. Still more critter-brand egregiousness and punning, in this case from South Africa's Fairview Winery, which has also introduced a "Goat Roti" and a "Bored Doe."

4. Chat-en-Oeuf. The Cleveland Amory–ization of wine. Yet another critter pun, this time on behalf of a cheap Languedoc red made by a French concern that's trying to mimic the New Worlders. Comes with literalistic label depicting—wait for it—a cat sitting on an egg.

5. Cat's Pee on a Goosebury Bush. A funny-enough Oz Clarke description of a Sauvignon

Blanc loses all cred when repurposed as the name for this plonk from New Zealand, which, after Australia, is the worst offender in the precious-label stakes.

6. The Little Penguin. Australian maker of cheap, nonvintage wines—evidently, given the adorable bird on the label, for children.

7. Woop Woop. Australian winery known for its decent Shiraz, if not its cleverness.

8. Mia's Playground. A line of wines from California's Don Sebastiani & Sons (Mia is Don's now-grown daughter), which has taken precious branding to alarming extremes; they also have a screwtop line called Screw Kappa Napa and a luxury blend called Used Automobile Parts.

9. Folie à Deux. Napa Valley pioneer in precious labeling, founded in the 1980s by two psychiatrists with a fondness for swirly watercolors.

10. The Poet. High-end Cabernet blend from Napa Valley's Cosentino Winery. Big, balanced, luscious . . . and utterly embarrassing to order.

Denominazione di Origine Controllata (DOC). Italian analog to the French AOC classification system, put in place in the early 1960s in order to make Italy more of a player in the Snob-wine race. In the early 1980s, after complaints from winemakers that the Italian government had been too promiscuous with its handouts of DOC appellations, there was introduced a more exclusive designation, *Denominazione di Origine Controllata e Garantita* (DOGC), which covers such blue-chip wines as Barolo, Barbaresco, and Brunello di Montalcino. It is a point of Snob pride to be fluent in these alphabet-soup gradations, as well as the more recently devised *Indicazione Geografica Tipica* (IGT), a catchall that covers such high-quality but non–DOC and DOGC wines as SUPER TUSCANS.

DRC. Snob shorthand for Domaine de la Romanée-Conti, the legendary but puny Burgundy estate whose vineyards, such as La Tâche and Richebourg, produce exquisite Grand CRU wines that are not so much prized as considered the culmination of the drinker's existential quest for truth. *It was after a sip of my first DRC, a '78 La Tâche, that I knew my life would never be the same.*

Draper, Paul. Gentle, professorially goateed wine-maker at Ridge Vineyards since 1969, and the man responsible for transforming a former workhorse grape, Zinfandel, into the most fetishized VARIETAL this side of Pinot Noir. In addition to making restrained, CLARET-like Zins that resist latter-day FRUIT BOMB trends, Draper and his team are  Snob-revered for their Cabernets and Bordeaux-style blends such as Monte Bello, the '71 vintage of which awed even the unsuspecting Frenchies at the JUDGMENT OF PARIS.

Paul Draper

Dry-farmed. Adjective applied to vines farmed without irrigation, which, while a risky practice in hot and dry climes, can lead to exceptionally CONCENTRATED wines, owing to the grapes' reduced water content and against-the-odds struggle to flourish. OLD-VINE vineyards best lend themselves to this approach, given that their gnarly old plants have deep taproots and a proven fortitude that inures them to the challenges of water stress. *An elegant and mathematically complex Zin made from* dry-farmed *vines planted in 1887...*

1855 classification. Snob shorthand for the Bordeaux Wine Official Classification of 1855, a ranking of the great wine region's CRUs that was commissioned by Napoléon III himself for that year's Exposition Universelle de Paris. This classification, much of which was cribbed from COCKS AND FÉRET's guidebook, continues to hold sway as the definitive ranking of Bordeaux's First through Fifth Growths—a circumstance that, as many a chagrined wine progressivist has noted, has allowed certain classified châteaux to coast on reputation for well over a century.

Enoteca. Italian word meaning "wine bar" or "wine shop," increasingly used in restaurant titles and signage by chef-proprietors eager to push Italy's ever-more-chic wines, often in 250-ml carafes tweely referred to as *quartinos.*

Enomatic. Italian-designed advance in wine gizmotology that extends the shelf life of wines in already-opened bottles. Somewhat resembling a self-serve soda machine at a McDonald's, the Enomatic, in its various formats,

Enomatic

holds several bottles, whose contents are dispensed through an airtight tap system; as the bottles empty, their open space is automatically filled with inert gas, preventing oxidation. An especially useful bit of technology for restaurants and wine bars specializing in FLIGHTS, and for wine shops that wish to offer the vintner's equivalent to a listening booth in a Virgin Megastore.

En primeur. Trade term for "wine futures," usually denoting those for high-end Bordeaux wines that are sold in cartel-like fashion by haughty merchants called *négociants.* At once rarified and vaguely sleazy, like the art world and MI5, the *en primeur* system is fueled by the BARREL-TASTING appraisals of journalists and merchants. Futures buyers don't receive the final, bottled products for several years, at which point they either flip them for profit or spirit them away to temperature-controlled cellars for long-term aging and caressing.

Epiphany wine. Any wine that, once tasted, is so utterly transporting and life-altering that it transforms a civilian into a full-on Wine Snob—and even, in extreme cases, into a Wine Snob who becomes a full-time wine professional. Both hobbyist and professional Snobs enjoy regaling colleagues with their epiphanic tales of discovery. *I was nineteen. I had a*

*girl with me. Father was away. I was forbidden to go
down into his cellar, but we did anyway, uncorked a bottle, and I took a swig that blew my mind. Can't remem-
ber the girl's name, but the wine was a '50 Lafleur—my*
epiphany wine.

EuroCave. French company specializing in the manu-
facture of climate-controlled wine cabinets, the presence
of which alongside a Sub–Zero fridge
and a Viking or Wolf range com-
pletes the nouveau-riche kitchen. For
those with endless space and re-
sources, EuroCave also offers elabo-
rate cellar racking systems and cigar
humidors.

EuroCave

Extract. The amount of solid material in a wine, a
greater presence of which makes the wine darker,
more viscous, and fuller of MOUTHFEEL. The in-
the-know Snob, rather than calling a wine "full-
bodied," uses the more modish "extracted."

Eye of the partridge. The single most eccentric phrase
in the professional taster's arsenal, describing not a
flavor but a shade of pink ascribed to good rosé
Champagne. A flowery remnant of an earlier, more
genteel, more English-dominated era of Wine
Snobbery.

Finigan, Robert. Agreeable, Harvard-educated Bay Area wine writer and restaurant critic whose eponymous private newsletter covered the Napa-Sonoma oeno-revolution of the 1970s and '80s in real time, and whose low-key charm made him an unlikely swordsman of said movement. Embroiled for a time in the early '80s in a bitter, Yankees–Red Sox–style rivalry with ROBERT PARKER, Finigan today soldiers on as an author of populist, wine-for-everyone books.

Finish. Snob term for "aftertaste." A wine's greatness is considered to be proportionate to the length of its finish. ROBERT PARKER actually includes the length of a wine's finish in his ratings, usually measured in seconds, but sometimes, in especially Snobworthy moments, in minutes.

Flabby. Pejorative for a wine of low acidity, suggesting it was made from overripe grapes or subjected to market-driven manipulations. *It has a decent nose, but it's flat and* flabby *on the palate.*

Flight. A thematic tasting of different wines in succession, as served in *ENOTECAS* and other venues where the staff and ownership are precious about wine. A flight-style sampler is often also a showcase for a bartender or sommelier's putative genius for food-wine pairings. *So, we've got a nice three-stage Oregon Pinot flight here, which I've matched with a wedge of local cheddar, some marcona almonds, and a salmon–goat cheese wonton.*

Flying winemakers. Formerly innocuous term for Southern Hemisphere winery hands who migrated annually from Australia and New Zealand to France and Italy, the better to see how the OLD WORLD–sters did things and stay elbow-deep in JUICE all year round. More recently, the term has come to be applied, with apprehension and hand-wringing, to the growing multitude of overcompensated celebrity consultants as exemplified by MICHEL ROLLAND.

Food-friendly. Olive-branch term used by Snobs when they're in the magnanimous mood to engage non-Snobs. Usually denotes a well-made but "simple" wine that matches up easily with whatever some polo-shirted weekend grillmeister is cooking up out back. *And the great thing is, Rieslings are so food-friendly that you can drink 'em with poached salmon, grilled chicken . . . even your famous shrimp kebabs, Brad.*

François Frères. French *tonnellerie* (cooperage) that makes the barrels in which the most esteemed

Burgundian winemakers, including all the DRC labels, age their product. Snobs pride themselves on knowing that the family-run firm uses oak primarily from the Tronçais forest in central France, whose trees produce a tight-grained wood that, when toasted just so, magnificently enhances a wine's COMPLEXITY. François Frères barrels are also used by aspirational NEW WORLD winemakers who can afford their tab, among them Au Bon Climat's JIM CLENDENEN, who went so far as to name his son Knox, after the cooperage's U.S. barrel broker, Mel Knox.

Fruit bomb. Modern-style purplish-red wine valued for its big, jammy flavor above all other considerations, such as STRUCTURE and long-term aging potential. The blame/credit for fruit bombs, which Snobs regard as crass, slutty "drink now" wines that don't warrant serious consideration, is usually attributed to Australia, whose winemakers discovered a ready market in the 1990s for young Syrahs (or Shiraz wines, in OZ parlance) that taste like grape-infused butane.

Fussy Pussy. Insiderist vulgarism for Pouilly-Fuissé, the white Burgundy. An unlikely borrowing from stoner comic Cheech Marin, who requested "some of that Fussy Pussy" in the landmark Cheech & Chong film *Nice Dreams*.

Gaja, Angelo. Regal, slicked-back *duce* of Italian wine, known for his exquisite Barolos and Barbarescos adorned with austere black-and-white labels and priced in the same range as used Volvos and new MacBooks. A lionized figure given to theatrically Italian pronouncements, Gaja, who was born in 1940 to a Piemontese family that's been in the wine business since 1859, muscled his way into the global wine elite well before most of his late-to-the-party Italian brethren, and has been making "modern," *BARRIQUE*-aged wines of profound STRUCTURE since taking the reins of the business in the 1960s.

Angelo Gaja

Gambero Rosso. Italian wine review published by the editorial wing of Slow Food, the righteous organization-movement founded by the polemicist and ardent localista Carlo Petrini. Oddly, given Slow Food's agrarian socialist leanings, *Gambero* looks kindly upon ultramodern, "international" wines with no apparent sense of place, often bestowing upon them its highest rating of *tre bicchieri,* or "three glasses." While some dissenters regard *Gambero* as more corruptible than most wine guides because of its

Italianness, its publication is nonetheless an event for Italo-Snobs.

Garagiste. Frenchified term for an artisanal wine producer whose output is so small that his whole outfit is housed in his garage, or at least a building as small as a garage. Garagiste wines, no matter what their quality, are coveted by Snobs for the insiderist cachet they carry, and are thus usually scandalously overpriced. Though the typical garagiste wine comes from Napa or Sonoma, the movement's spiritual home is Château Valandraud, one of the many tiny, antiestablishment properties in Bordeaux that wowed ROBERT PARKER with small-production, ultra-EXTRACTED wines aged in *BARRIQUE.*

Garrigue. French term for the fragrant scrubland of southern France, particularly the Provence region, which has seduced countless gastro- and oeno-tourists in the travel-boom decades since World War II. Used to evoke rusticity and pastoral idylls, and generally applied to earthy, fragrant Rhône and Provençal wines. *While the bistro's sturdy Maman prepared our meal, the bald, convivial Papa ambled to our table with a humble but pleasing* vin du table, *its nose perfumed with the lavender and herbs of the* garrigue.

Grand Award. Distinction bestowed by the *Wine Spectator* upon those restaurants with the lengthiest, most Snobworthy wine lists in the world; fewer than a hundred establishments have been deemed worthy. Among the hallmarks of a Grand Award–winning restaurant are a list offering upward of 1,500 wines, an abundance of big bottles and VERTICALS, an A-list sommelier whose travels are underwritten by a wealthy backer, and a late-night scene populated by serious collectors and other A-list sommeliers, who can be espied through windows after hours sticking their noses into balloon glasses. *Knock my ambition all you want, but two restaurants in my hospitality group have* Grand Award *status, which is more than you can say for your places, beeyatch!*

Grape, the. Exceptionally pretentious synonym for *wine* or *things related to wine*; favored by Snobs prone to pontification. *Son, allow me to school you in the ways of* the grape.

Gravner, Josko. Winemaking primitivist who runs an eccentric operation in the northeastern Italian region of Friuli. A godhead of the ZERO MANIPULATION cult, Gravner, a repentant former high-techist, celebratedly ferments his wine in large, beeswax-lined clay amphorae that are buried to their necks in the earth, as was done in the Bronze Age. Shunning persnickety temperature-control monitors and allowing the juice to stay in contact with skins and other solids for several months, Gravner essentially lets his wines make themselves, producing a unique and polarizing product. His whites, for which he is best known, are cloudy, copper-colored, and highly oxidative in flavor, leaving amateurs to wonder why they're being served cider and giving independent-minded Snobs a cause célèbre to be evangelical about.

Green. Pejorative slang term for an underripe wine, usually a red, that has flavors of green bell peppers and/or other salad produce. To suggest that a wine is green is to intimate that its grapes were harvested too soon, picked from young vines, or the product of a poor vintage, all high crimes in the court of the Snob. *It had a decent concentration, but I couldn't get past how* green *it was on the nose.*

Grip. Sensation ascribed to a wine with enough acidity and/or TANNIN that it seems to actually grab hold of the palate. Considered a good thing by Snobs. *The '75 had powerhouse tannins and a marvelous* grip *at first, but it lost its resolve as it got more air.*

Grower Champagne. A small-batch sparkling wine that is not only made from grapes grown in the Champagne region, as all wines carrying the designation must be, but produced and bottled on the very estates where the grapes are grown; the Champagne equivalent of a "farmstead" cheese. While the mass-market luxury brands incorporate brought-in grapes from various other estates, grower Champagne (also known as small-grower Champagne) is the only Champagne truly redolent of *TERROIR*, and therefore the Snob choice for special occasions. *We celebrated New Year's with a magnificent Egly-Ouriet, a* grower Champagne *with a sassy Pinot push.*

Gunflint. Tasting term used to suggest steely MINERALITY, especially in crisp, dry Chablis wines, whose grapes are grown in soil rich with limestone and fossilized-seashell matter. Lyrical as the term is, it's more intuitive than experiential; rare is the Snob who has actually licked an antique flintlock gun.

A BLUFFER'S GUIDE
TO VARIETAL
CLICHÉ-SPEAK

When tasting a . . .	*You can't go wrong describing it as . . .*
Sauvignon Blanc	grassy
Syrah	peppery
Chablis	minerally*
Barolo	earthy
Southern Rhône red	spicy
American Chardonnay	buttery
Cabernet Sauvignon	cassis-like
Zinfandel	jammy
Riesling	steely
Muscadet	flinty
Malbec	tarry

NOTE: Pinot Noir has been deliberately omitted from this list because Wine Snobs celebrate it as the one grape whose complexity defies easy description—especially by the likes of you.

*Not, technically, a real word.

Hang time. NEW WORLD, doobage-redolent descriptive term for the length of a growing season and, therefore, how long grapes hang on the vine before harvest; a longer hang time implies greater depth of flavor, the antithesis of GREEN. *People bitch about the fog here in Santa Maria, but that's the great thing about this place, man—it refreshes the vines and lets us push the* hang time.

Harlan Estate. Ultimate cult winery, located in Napa and founded by real-estate developer and shrewd Snob-manipulator Bill Harlan. Harlan's mailing-list-only, $300-a-bottle "estate wine," a Bordeaux-style red crafted with help from the jet-setting consultant MICHEL ROLLAND, is more gossiped about than tasted—prompting feverish bidding whenever it pops up at such wealth-flaunting spectacles as the Napa Valley Wine Auction, held at the Harlan-built Meadowood Resort.

Harlan Estate

Harmony. Florid synonym for BALANCE, suggestive not just of equilibrium in wine but of a musical mingling of flavors and textures—yea, verily, like notes in a chord. *The luscious peach-scented fruit is in exquisite* harmony *with the racy, mineral acidity.*

Heitz, Joe. Irascible Napa Valley pioneer (1919–2000) known for his steely glare, short fuse, and awesome Cabernets. Armed with a master's degree from UC-DAVIS's wine program, Heitz worked under ANDRE TCHELISTCHEFF before striking out on his own in 1961. An early practitioner of "ego pricing" (as emulated by Italy's ANGELO GAJA, among others), Heitz had the temerity to set prices in benchmark-Bordeaux range rather than in the then-cheap Napa range, and relished a good confrontation, once sending ROBERT PARKER a box of handkerchiefs after Parker wrote that a Heitz Cab had no aroma. (The implication being that

Parker clearly had a cold.) The fabled 1974 vintage of his Martha's Vineyard Cabernet—so named for a grape-grower in Oakville, California, not for Massachusetts's Danson-Steenburgen summer playground—is a Snob-revered EPIPHANY WINE.

Joe Heitz

Hermacinski, Ursula. Adorable and charismatic (by wine-world standards) auctioneer, known as "the goddess of the gavel" since *Food & Wine* magazine nicknamed her thusly. Hermacinski first commanded Snob attention at the 1992 NAPA VALLEY WINE

AUCTION, a wine-dork fest whose auctioneers had previously been men, where she charmed the crowd with her flirty banter and efficient JUICE-trafficking. Now in charge of the wine-auction department at Zachy's, the high-end Westchester County (NY) wine retailer, Hermacinski is especially in demand on the charity circuit, where her presence alone draws crowds of moony, excitable Snob collectors.

Hot. Counterintuitively pejorative term (to Paris Hilton, anyway) for a wine that is inordinately high in alcohol, leading to a burning, unpleasant FINISH. An increasingly heard criticism in a FRUIT BOMB era of alcohol levels at or approaching 15 or 16 percent. *Blechh, that Syrah was so* hot *that I couldn't enjoy any food with it.*

THE EPIPHANY-WINE SHORT LIST: A TOP TEN FOR WOULD-BE SNOBS

There's no Snob exercise more fraught than the compilation (and declamation) of one's "all-time" list of life-changing wines—especially when you're put on the spot by your father-in-law, your boss, or a collection of dandruffy wine writers gathered in some woody Napa juice joint. How best to convey one's oeno-cultural supremacy in a mere ten selections, without resorting (entirely) to cliché and flagrant label whoredom? Herewith, a ten-pack of irrefutable Snob greats that will pass muster with connoisseurs and poseurs alike.

Case Basse di Soldera Brunello di Montalcino Riserva 1990

Château Cheval-Blanc 1947 (or the '82)

Château Rayas Châteauneuf-du-Pape 1990

Domaine de la Romanée–Conti La Tâche
1971

Giacomo Conterno Barolo Monfortino
1978

Heitz Martha's Vineyard Napa Valley
Cabernet Sauvignon 1974

Jaboulet Hermitage La Chapelle 1978 (or
the '61 or the '90)

Jayer Cros Parantoux 1985

Tenuta San Guido Sassicaia 1985

Vega Sicilia "Unico" 1970

Indigenous. Adjective whose meaning—"originating in a particular place"—has taken on an emotional dimension in the minds of Snobs passionate about *TERROIR* and wary of globalization and homogenization. *Why would I drink a Sicilian Merlot with all that killer* indigenous *stuff they have there?*

Inglenook. Sullied name of once-noble Napa Valley winery, now better associated, thanks to the company's having passed through a series of corporate owners, with cheap jug PLONK and sweet "blush" wines for minivan moms. Originally built in the 1880s by a Finnish fur trader named Gustave Niebaum, the Inglenook estate began to thrive in the 1930s under the direction of Niebaum's great-nephew John Daniel Jr., making California's first great Cabernets. It continued to do so until the early 1960s ('40s-era Inglenook Cabs still evoke heavy panting at auction), when Daniel sold the company and it was reconceived as a mass-market brand. Years later, the filmmaker Francis Ford Coppola, himself no stranger to epic tales of fallen empires, acquired the original Inglenook property and restored it to its former glory, renaming its on-site winery Niebaum-Coppola, and more recently re-renaming it Rubicon. *I've still got some '45 Inglenook in my cellar and it's showing like a champ right now!*

"IT'S FANTASTIC, AND NO ONE KNOWS ABOUT IT!"

Keeping the Good Snob Wines
Straight from the Crap

Wine Snobs relish the opportunity to buck conventional wisdom and make the case that some discredited or obscure genre of fermented grape juice (or related alcoholic beverage) is actually awesome, a *wine experience* that the timid Merlot herds just don't "get." Yet for every credible cause célèbre, like the justly rehabilitated rosé, there is a clunker—"Txakoli is the next Chablis, mark my words!"—that seems to have been singled out for unwarranted praise just because some Snob wanted to make his colleagues feel ignorant and close-minded. Herewith, a consumer's guide to Snob trustworthiness.

Ten Worthwhile Snob Causes Célèbres

Sherry

Port

Rosé

Austrian Grüner Veltliner

Italian Lagrein

Hungarian Tokaji

German Trockenbeerenauslese

Clare Valley Riesling (Australia)

Grower Champagne

Argentine Malbec

Ten Fraudulent Snob Causes Célèbres

Cava

Sake

Lambrusco

Austrian Zweigelt

"Cal-Italians" (wines produced in
   California from Italian varietals)

South African Pinotage

Swiss Chasselas

Txakoli

Primitivo

Long Island Riesling

Johnnes, Daniel. Whippersnapper prodigy turned East Coast wine authority of the Francophilic old school. Making his name in the late 1980s as the boy sommelier of Montrachet in New York, Johnnes matured into an internationally known author and wine importer, a diminutive yet intimidating presence at tastings. While his squinty, withering stare evokes Clint Eastwood at a gunfight, he's apt to initiate the uninitiated by benignly asking "What do you like about that wine?"

Johnson, Hugh. Irreverent, beetle-browed Brit wine authority, known to mere enthusiasts for his eponymous yearly pocket guides, but worthy of Snob consideration by dint of his encyclopedic publishing debut, simply entitled *Wine* (1966), his *World Atlas of Wine* (originally published in 1971), and his disdain for ROBERT PARKER, whom Johnson has likened to George W. Bush and assigned the epithet "the dictator of taste in Baltimore." Cheekier than most of wine's Brit Pack—he was educated, like John Cleese, at Cambridge University, and born the same year, 1939—Johnson

Hugh Johnson

is a man unafraid to offer that a Sauvignon Blanc can be either "austere or buxom."

Judgment of Paris. Landmark 1976 blind tasting of French and California wines in which the nine judges, all of them French, voted a Napa Valley Chardonnay as the best of the whites and a Napa Cabernet Sauvignon as the best of the reds. The tasting, held in Paris and arranged by a young English wineshop owner named Steven Spurrier, is considered the signal moment in which California wines "arrived," thereby paving the way for the state's oeno-industry boom, an explosion of boutique wineries with the gall to charge $60 for a Petite Sirah, and sky-rocketing real-estate prices in Napa and Sonoma that forced locals who'd lived in those counties for generations to move elsewhere.

Juice. Grating hipster term for wine, used especially in the San Francisco Bay Area, where younger, ostensibly hipper Snobs in the wine trade think that, by referring to wine as such, they are demystifying it for a grateful audience of Francophobes and reg'lar folk who will feel less intimidated if they think of wine as fermented grape juice. Except the very deployment of such insiderist terms serves only to intimidate civilians all over again.

Kerosene. Tasting term applied to Rieslings, usually flatteringly; used interchangably in Britain with *petrol.* For Wine Snobs, a belated justification for childhood huffing sessions at gas stations and Agway stores.

Kopec, Tim. Shaggy-haired compiler and overseer of the GRAND AWARD–winning list at Veritas, a small New York restaurant purpose-built as a Wine Snob mecca and singled out for praise by pretend-dangerous food personality Anthony Bourdain in his book *Kitchen Confidential.* By dint of being more cerebral and less shticky than his fellow sommeliers, Kopec has cultivated a mystique among Wine Snobs akin to that which surrounds Thomas Keller, the unknowable chef-godhead of the French Laundry, in Food Snob circles.

La-La's, the. Cloying sobriquet for a trio of extraordinarily expensive Côte-Rôtie reds—La Mouline, La Turque, and La Landonne—produced in eye-dropper quantities by the Rhône Valley stalwart Guigal. Given the tininess of both the source vineyards and their yield (about 200 cases of each wine per year), the La-La's inspire breathless auction-house chatter and frenzied, elbow-checking positioning among high-end merchants. In this light, the childlike term itself is especially unpleasant to hear coming from a Snob's lips, like a billionaire oilman's baby talk to his mistress. *An '83 La Mouline? Ooh, me likey this silky, sexy* La-La!

La-La's

Leather. Tasting term applied to complex red wines, usually flatteringly. For Wine Snobs, a belated justification for childhood oral fixations that involved book-bag straps and/or fringed cowboy vests.

Lichine, Alexis. Dapper, aristocratic, White Russian wine expert (1913–1989), credited with teaching flush postwar Americans to appreciate fine French wines while simultaneously pushing reluctant French winemakers to actually market their product to *les Américains stupides.* Best known for two authoritative books, *The Wines of France* (1951) and *Alexis Lichine's Encyclopedia of Wines & Spirits* (1967), Lichine, whose family fled the Russian Revolution, initially made his name in the United States as FRANK SCHOONMAKER's deputy, and later ran his own importing company and his own Bordeaux estate, Château Prieuré-Lichine. A pomaded playboy, Lichine also achieved status as a Hollywood-gossip footnote by being one of the many husbands of the 1950s starlet and serial marrier Arlene Dahl.

Alexis Lichine

Lynch, Kermit. Berkeley wine merchant and oenological counterpart to Chez Panisse earth-mother Alice Waters in the Bay Area's gastro-oenological Age of Aquarius. Besotted, like Waters, with an imagined ideal of southern France, Lynch embarked in the early 1970s on a wine-buying excursion to Provence, took one whiff of the *GARRIGUE,* and never looked back. Abetted by the expat cookbook author and Food Snob godhead Richard Olney, who served as his translator and *consigliere,* Lynch brought back and sold quirky selections that, by dint of their placement at Chez Panisse, became Boomer Snob favorites. The author of several Franco-rhapsodic books that make even Peter Mayle look like a piker (the most famous of which is *Adventures on the Wine Route,* a staple on the Snob shelf), Lynch still keeps a mellow-vibe wine shop in Berkeley, immediately adjacent to Waters's breakfast-lunch spot Café Fanny.

Malolactic fermentation. A controlled fermentation process that occurs after the primary alcoholic fermentation, in which a winemaker adds special bacterial cultures so that malic acid is converted to lactic acid, resulting in a reduction of the wine's sharp, crisp qualities and a greater softness, creaminess, and complexity. The results of *malo,* as this process is sometimes called by Snobs, are more noticeable in white wines than in red. *I'm getting stone fruits, cashews, and nice toastiness on this Chardonnay, with good* malo *influence and a buttery finish.*

Mascarello, Bartolo. Lovable, Yoda-like Italian vintner-patriarch (1927–2005) known for dispensing wisdom to generations of pilgrims who journeyed to his farmstead in the Piedmontese village of Barolo. Revered for his earthy, acidic Barolo, which, to some Italophile Snobs, represents the ultimate in pure VARIETAL expression (and is now made by his daughter, Maria-Teresa), Mascarello, who vaguely resembled Uncle Junior from *The Sopranos,* held forth in later years from his wheelchair—parked in a tiny *ufficio* without telephones or computers—and inveighed to a sympathetic audience against the evils of *BARRIQUES* and technological winemaking.

Master Sommelier. Official designation bestowed by the London-based Court of Master Sommeliers, a secretive, J. K. Rowling–evocative organization, formed in the 1960s, whose rigorous examination may be taken only by invitation, and for an $800 fee at that. Stingy with its approval, the Court only allows thirteen applicants per year to take the test, and has granted the Master Sommelier designation (which its holders shorten to "MS" and append to their names as a suffix, like "PhD") to fewer than 150 people. Those who take the test must vow not to divulge the details of its most rigorous phase, which involves not guessing vintages or showcasing one's knowledge of obscure Grüner Vetliners, but weathering abuse from Court members playacting as especially unpleasant customers.

Meritage. Deceptively French-sounding American term, propagated by a group of Napa Valley winemakers in the 1980s to serve as a pseudoclassification (and registered trademark) for Bordeaux-style blended wines that can't use VARIETAL labeling but are too good to be sold as mere "table wine." A combination of the words *merit* and *heritage,* meritage is meant to rhyme with the latter word, but is often Frenchified by clueless would-be Snobs into "meri-*tahj,*" lending further Euroflash cred to such luxe wines like Opus One and Insignia. *The '03 Viader Napa Valley Red* Meritage *strikes a deliciously harmo-*

nious balance between the Cabernets Franc and Sauvignon.

Microclimate. Meteorological-agricultural term that, when applied by a Snob to a confined grape-growing space, takes on a spiritual dimension. Useful in reverently describing the discrete characteristics of a particular CRU, e.g., *Those higher-elevation vineyards have a cooler* microclimate, *which gives the grapes more hang time and a better ability to tell the story of those old hills.*

Micro-oxygenation. Catchall, cure-all winemaking technique hustled by highly paid consultants of the MICHEL ROLLAND ilk. The process involves introducing small, measured amounts of oxygen into a wine while it is still in a fermentation tank, a manipulation that results in softer tannins, deeper color, and a more NEW WORLD style. Hailed as a brilliant advance in winemaking at the time of its introduction in the early 1990s, the process is now decried by *TERROIR*-ists, who regard it with horror and cringe at a certain sequence in the film *MONDOVINO*—in which Rolland emerges from his chauffered sedan and advises several different clients to use the process—as if watching the horse's-head scene in *The Godfather.*

Mid-palate. Snob shorthand for the middle part of the wine-tasting experience, between the ATTACK and the FINISH, where the taster gets a sense of a wine's body and overall STRUCTURE—and, therefore, its viability as a "serious" wine. *This Pinot was promising enough up front, but it fell flat on the* mid-palate.

Minerality. Term for the perceived mineral content in a wine, suggesting in its user an implausibly intimate knowledge of the *TERROIR* in which the grapes are grown. Frequently used by professional tasters eager to showboat their inner geologist. *This is a racy, soil-driven Sauvignon, with a flinty* minerality *that roots it in the Kimmeridgian limestone of Sancerre.*

Mondavi, Robert. Hard-driving, Grecophile potentate of the American wine industry (1913–2008) and protagonist in a dynastic epic of Shakespearian dimensions. The forceful, jockish son of an Italian immigrant turned California grape-seller, Mondavi acrimonously split in the 1960s with his family—whose stewardship of the Charles Krug Winery struck him as unambitious and too jug-wine-ish in the old UC-DAVIS style—and proceeded to build an empire based on the simultaneous courting of the high (Opus One) and low (Woodbridge) ends of the Snob spectrum. A later round of familial dysfunction, involving tensions between his sons, led Mondavi to sell his operations to the corporate wine monster Constellation Brands in 2004. (Charles Krug, on the other hand, is still owned by the family of his brother, Peter, with whom Robert reconciled only when both men hit their nineties.) Still, Mondavi remained a Napa Valley institution, admired for his philanthropy, his instrumental role in California's oeno-gastronomical evolution, and the status he commanded, with his aggressively blond wife, Margrit, as the Bob and Dolores Hope of Napa Valley.

Robert Mondavi

Mondovino. Amateurishly shot documentary film, released in 2004, in which the wine-loving director, Jonathan Nossiter, spans the globe to mount a defense of small, ostensibly artisanal wine producers whose livelihoods are threatened by large, globalized, corporatized producers and the ROBERT PARKER–led internationalization of the palate. Upheld by Snobs as a truer and better film than the contemporaneous *Sideways,* which is merely misinformed twaddle for the arthouse masses; earns further Snob points for intimating that the best wines are made by angry communists with tiny plots and minimal technological apparatus.

Monopole. Patrician, prestigious term for a CRU controlled by a single owner—a relative rarity, given that, as dictated by typically baffling French inheritance laws, a vineyard is often broken up into several small parcels rather than preserved intact after a patriarch dies. A ready knowledge of the who's who of monopoles is a mark of advanced, graduate-level Wine Snobbery. While monopoles are not exclusive to Burgundy, they are most readily associated with the region—especially in the case of the exalted DRC, which boasts two monopole vineyards, Romanée-Conti and La Tâche.

Mouthfeel. Icky word, also beloved of Food Snobs, for the texture of a wine as it coats the tongue and palate. *Ooh, the tannins in this Cab are nicely developed—they give it a real velvety* mouthfeel.

Napa Valley Wine Auction. Colloquial term for the auction held every June by the Napa Valley Vintners trade association, which actually rather grandly calls the event "Auction Napa Valley—The American Classic." The premier "do" on the wealthy Snob collector's social calendar, the auction is an opportunity not only to pair cowboy boots with a tuxedo, but to best other Snobs in a CULT WINE–fueled, trophy-wife-cheered throwdown of frenzied bidding. Like most high-profile latter-day charity fundraisers, the auction, which costs $1,000 a head just to enter, is a lively mixture of do-gooding and metaphorical penis-measuring by venture capitalists, hedge-funders, tech moguls, and other assorted titans.

New World. Quaintly Columbian term used to describe wines produced outside of the "traditional" wine-growing regions of Western and Northern Europe. Though the United States is most readily identified with New World wines, the term also applies to the wines of Chile, Australia, and South Africa. New World wines are broadly thought of as fruitier and more alcoholic than OLD WORLD wines, owing to the hotter climates in which their grapes are grown and the preponderance of producers eager to please ROBERT PARKER.

🍷 **1961.** Landmark vintage for Bordeaux, rivaled only by 1982 as the most Snob-revered of the twentieth century. By virtue of being an earlier year, and therefore the rarer, more expensive vintage, 1961 is a de rigueur talking point for Snobs wishing to showcase their wealth, worldliness, and BROADBENT-like erudition. *I thought the Lynch-Bages was by far the best of the '61s we tasted.*

Nose. Snob term for "aroma," having supplanted the term *bouquet,* now used solely by old ladies and Englishmen. Though even fledgling Snobs deploy the term with ease as a noun—e.g., *This has an expressive* nose, *with hints of road tar and chamomile*—the truly hardcore use the word as a verb: *Shhh! Keep it down while I* nose *this juice.*

Oenology. Preferred Snob spelling of *enology,* because it reads as more forbiddingly English on the page—and because it leaves non-Snobs uncertain of how to pronounce it (EE-nology).

Old-vine. Romantic viticultural signifier for wines wrung from the scant output of *vieilles vignes,* as the French refer to the most aged of grape plants. An older vine produces less fruit, and is thought to have reserves of nutrients in its thick, gnarly trunk, resulting in more CONCENTRATED grapes. *When you drink those* old-vine *Ridge Zins, you're tasting history in a bottle, bro.*

Old World. Sepiatone–evocative term that refers chiefly to Continental Europe, the ancestral homeland of viticulture. As originally practiced by the British, Wine Snobbery was focused entirely on Old World wines, and while the rise of the NEW WORLD and ROBERT PARKER shifted the Snob paradigm, there remains a sizable Snob sector that still regards Old World favoritism as a mark of gentlemanliness and refinement. *I can't get my head around those high-alcohol California Pinots; my palate is really more attuned to the* Old World.

Over-oaked. Common Snob plaint during tastings, describing a wine whose maker has let the JUICE's flavor get overpowered by that of the barrel in which it was aged. Though some degree of oakiness is desirable in many wines, imparting toasty and/or vanilla-like qualities, the prevailing Snob lament is that the American palate favors big, unsubtle flavors, resulting in domestic wines that are deliberately made to taste like lumber. *His Chardonnay's okay, but his Sauvignon Blanc is so* over-oaked *that I hurled.*

Oidium. Nasty blight that covers the leaves of vines in a powdery gray mildew and dehydrates the grapes themselves, imparting a fungal "off" taste to wine made from them. Unlike *BOTRYTIS,* oidium doesn't need moisture to flourish and can strike in dry, seemingly perfect conditions. Wine history is pockmarked with 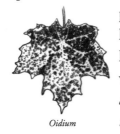 periodic oidium crises that, not unlike PHYLLOXERA infestations, have left Snobs longing for irretrievable vintages. *Oh, to have tasted a Madeira as Jefferson might have sipped, before the dread* oidium *struck.*

Oidium

Oz. Nickname for Australia, which, though widely used outside of a wine context, is especially cherished by Snobs who value the vinelands Down Under. *Just back from Oz, with the red earth of Barossa still on my bootsoles and the purple stain of old-vine Shiraz still on my tongue!*

Pain grillé. Amusingly Continental TASTING NOTES descriptor for a luxuriously oaked (albeit not OVER-OAKED) wine that might otherwise be saddled with the more pedestrian "toasty." *This Merlot delivers a classic perfume of* pain grillé, *smoke, espresso, and black currants.*

Parker, Robert. Baltimore lawyer–turned–global overlord of wine-rating, at once respected by Snobs for legitimizing oeno-fetishism via his *Wine Advocate* magazine (begun in 1978) and his books (in particular 1985's *Bordeaux,* since updated) and reviled for his power over winemakers, who, even in Europe, have tailored their product to suit his palate, which favors enormous, planet-sized, fruity, oaky, viscous, heavily EXTRACTED wines high in tannins and alcohol. Snobs especially love to bemoan Parker's 100-point rating scale for wines, which impels lay consumers to avoid anything with a score lower than 90, and use the term *Parkerize* to describe the process by which wines and consumer tastes have changed as a result of Parker's influence. *Let us turn now to*

Robert Parker

*Chianti Classico, the last refuge of gracious, light, un-*Parkerized *Italian reds.*

Parr, Rajat. Calcutta-born celebrity sommelier who apprenticed under LARRY STONE and now oversees the wine operations of the aggressively expansionist San Francisco–based chef-restaurateur Michael Mina. Soft-spoken and less cult-inspiring than other sommeliers, Parr nevertheless hits the appropriate Snob marks—a juggernaut wine list of GRAND AWARD dimensions; an exhaustive expertise in Burgundy; a sideline as a hobby winemaker—and, as per Snob form, is knowingly referred to by a nickname ("Raj") rather than his full name.

Pencil lead. Improbably precise and toxic-sounding bit of TASTING NOTES phraseology, used to describe dark, tannic reds.

Pérignon, Dom. Seventeenth-century winemaker and Benedictine monk ("Dom" being the honorific, Pierre his actual name) folklorically credited with having invented Champagne. Although the discovery of sparkling wine was more likely a happy accident—most wines of that era likely underwent a spontaneous and unintentional second fermentation in the bottle—the Pérignon myth has been perpetuated by market-savvy producers, particularly the prescient Champagne monolith Moët & Chandon, which slapped the Dom's name on its top bottling in 1936, decades before "branding" or hip-hop existed.

Peynaud, Émile. Bordeaux oenologist (1912–2004) whose viticultural and technological winemaking innovations command such awe that his first name, like that of the great chef Escoffier, has been rendered superfluous. A professor at the Bordeaux Institute of Enology, Peynaud consulted for such heavy hitters as Châteaux Margaux and Lafite, while also serving as mentor to MICHEL ROLLAND and perfecting the technique of controlled MALOLACTIC FERMENTATION. Peynaud's exhaustive monograph, *Le Goût du Vin* (*The Taste of Wine*), is the definitive text on wine-tasting, employing charts, graphs, and even illustrations of the tongue's papillae to educate the Snob palate.

Phylloxera. Tiny, aphidlike pest native to North America that feeds on and infests the roots of grapevines, ultimately killing them. Inadvertently introduced into Europe in the 1800s, phylloxera destroyed two-thirds of the continent's vineyards by the end of the century, thereby creating a Wine Snob mythos of a vanished Eden whose scant extant bottlings sell at auction for astounding sums. *How cool is Broadbent for having tasted all those pre-*phylloxera *wines?*

Phylloxera

Pie spices. Tasting term applied to rich white wines and earthy California reds, usually to denote some putatively autumnal, nutmeggy quality. *Whoa, give this baby some air and you'll get the full, blossoming orgy of cola, smoke, mocha, and* pie spices.

Pipi de chat. Old-fashioned descriptive phrase, meaning "cat's piss" in French, that was used in a positive context when whiffing a white Sancerre or any other Sauvignon Blanc–based wine. Outmoded, but still wheeled out occasionally by Snobs to shock novitiates.

Pliny the Elder. First-century Roman naturalist and sage who meticulously cataloged his era's viticulture before ash from Vesuvius interred him in Pompeii. A figure deeply romanticized by the sort of Snob rhap-

Pliny the Elder

sodist who actually likes to utter the words *"In vino veritas"* aloud, Pliny is reliably cited in discussions of rustic, southern-Italian wines fashioned from indigenous grapes that date from his time—and often boast that as their sole selling point.

Plonk. British slang for cheap, low-quality wine, often used to self-deprecating effect when recalling one's pre-Snob days. *We used to take our dates to checkered-tablecloth joints, gettin' ourselves right pissed on* plonk *from straw-covered bottles.*

Prial, Frank. Durable, plainspoken *New York Times* wine columnist emeritus. A hardscrabble reporter on the paper's Metro desk, Prial accidentally became a wine writer in the early 1970s when he mentioned to *Times* culture czar Arthur Gelb that he liked THE GRAPE. Tapped to be the paper's wine expert, with a weekly column called "Wine Talk," Prial positioned himself as the anti-Snob, inveighing against the scourge of winespeak and recommending $5.99 bottles of Sutter Home Zinfandel when he felt like it— which, paradoxically, only enhanced his Snob cred. Since retiring from the column, he has specialized in writing *Times* obits and appreciations of recently deceased oeno-legends.

Priming. Showy glassware treatment in which a small amount of a just-decanted wine is sloshed around in each of the glasses it is to be served in, so as to coat the walls of the glasses with wine and neutralize potential taste contaminants (e.g., dishwasher detergent). A common wine-steward practice in high-end restaurants, priming nevertheless confuses novice Snobs, who think they're being presented with unwashed glasses from someone else's table.

A SHORT PRONUNCIATION GUIDE TO SNOB-ESTEEMED WINES, PERSONAGES, AND THINGS

Boh-la-ZHAY: Bollinger, venerable Champagne house

Angelo GUY-a: Angelo Gaja, posh Piedmontese winemaker

GUR-gitch Hills: Grgich Hills, Napa maker of celebrated Chardonnays

Koh-dree-UH: Condrieu, luscious Rhône white

Château dee-KHEM: Château d'Yquem, king of all Sauternes

Château Pay-TRUCE: Château Pétrus, unaffordable luxury Pomerol

Château traw-te-NWAH: Château Trotanoy, somewhat affordable luxury Pomerol

KROOG: Krug, Champagne house owned by the luxury conglomerate LVMH

Frank PRY-el: Frank Prial, stalwart, sensible *New York Times* wine writer

REED-el: Riedel, Austrian manufacturer of precious stemware

ROTES-shield: Rothschild, many-tentacled European banking family and multiple-Bordeaux-châteaux owners

ON-dray CHELL-a-cheff: André Tchelistcheff, Lilliputian visionary at Beaulieu Vineyards

Terry THEECE: Terry Theise, elfin promoter of German and Austrian wines

TIN-ya-NELL-o: Tignanello, modish Super Tuscan from Antinori

Will-LAM-it Valley: Willamette Valley, Pinot-intensive Oregon wine region

Quaffable. Backhanded Snob compliment for an agreeable yet simple wine. Sometimes used interchangeably with *drinkable,* though the latter term more precisely denotes approachability—e.g., *This Cab is* drinkable *now, though it will reward a decade or more of cellaring*—than mere acceptability. *For your daughter's wedding reception, I have a perfectly* quaffable *Côtes-du-Rhône at ten bucks a bottle, eight if you order six cases or more.*

Racy. Snob synonym for "crisp," most often deployed for Sauvignon Blancs and other high-acid whites. *I am so over all that butter and oak, man—gimme something food-friendly, with some nice* racy *acidity.*

Rhône Rangers. Fun-loving cadre of California wine-makers, anchored by the whimsical Randall Grahm of Bonny Doon, who, in the 1980s, championed the cultivation of Rhône Valley grapes such as Grenache and Syrah in the Golden State. The Rangers' Rhône-inspired bottlings, such as Grahm's pioneering Le Cigare Volant, gave Snobs a New Cool Thing to pursue after they'd tired of the Californian standbys Cabernet and Chardonnay, and effectively introduced the word *spicy* into the Snob vernacular.

Riedel. Fastidious Austrian glassware manufacturer whose ultra-delicate wineglasses are not merely elegant tableware but, according to the company's promotional materials, "precision tools in the service of wine." Though the Riedel family has been making glass products since the mid-eighteenth century, it didn't become a major player in the wine world until the 1970s, when it began to confer with winemakers and writers in order to anticipate Snob wants and needs. Designed with thin, "cut" rims to facilitate the proper distribution of wine across the palate, and available in myriad shapes custom-designed for specific wine styles, Riedel glasses promise a lifetime of sensual and intellectual satisfaction to those who can avoid breaking them after a single use.

Robinson, Jancis. Bespectacled, prolific British wine writer, best known for editing the *Oxford Companion to Wine,* the most scholarly of wine reference books and one often referred to in Snob shorthand as "Jancis"—e.g., *Look it up in* Jancis. Blessed with an authentic wit and an assuring sensible tone, which she puts to use in several shorter books, a

Financial Times column, a Web site, and sundry British "programmes," Robinson is also the lust object of several Wine Snob admirers, Jay McInerney among them, who harbor Miss Moneypenny fantasies about her.

Jancis Robinson

Rolland, Michel. Celebrity winemaking consultant, based in Bordeaux but forever flying first class to Chile, Argentina, Italy, and wherever else there are deep-pocketed vineyard owners willing to pay through the nose for his services. Demonized, like pal ROBERT PARKER, for strait-

Michel Rolland

jacketing viticultural variety and encouraging the wine world's absorption by corporate interests, Rolland was portrayed as a villain in *MONDOVINO*.

Route 29. California state highway that contracts into a relatively bucolic two-lane road as it runs through Napa Valley, with vineyards visible to the east and west. Usually spoken of dismissively by Snobs, who consider it a vulgar thoroughfare for tour buses and packs of drunken junior litigators in hired stretch limos. *Veered off onto the Silverado Trail to get away from the hellish masses on* Route 29.

Ruby. Go-to color descriptor for fine red wines, often deployed in hyphenate form, e.g., *purple*-ruby, ruby-*black,* ruby-*brown.* Connotes luxury and youthful vigor in TASTING NOTES, in marked contrast to the BRICK hue of older or lesser red wines.

Sassicaia. Aristocratic Tuscan red wine from the vaunted Tenuta San Guido estate, invented by the well-heeled hobby winemaker Marquis Mario Incisa della Rocchetta. A devoted aesthete and Bordeaux fiend, the Marquis brought back Cabernet Sauvignon cuttings from France in the 1940s, planted them, bottled his wine for family and friends in the '50s, and finally went commercial in the late '60s, rolling out the first pricey Italian wine to be considered a SUPER TUSCAN. Like DRC or Lafite, Sassicaia (still produced by the family of the Marquis, who died in 1983) has metamorphosed into a catchy byword for high status, a circumstance abetted by its fun-to-say name, which rolls off the tongues even of drunken bond traders.

Schoonmaker, Frank. Buccaneering, self-taught American wine writer and merchant (1905–1976) who wrested the very concept of oeno-expertise from Europhile Snobs, thereby paving the way for NEW WORLD Wine Snobbery. Best remembered today for his *Encyclopedia of Wine,* originally published in 1965 and still a staple of Snob reference shelves,

Schoonmaker was also a pioneer importer of Burgundys and, in his capacity as a consultant for several California wineries, the popularizer of the U.S. custom of identifying wines by their predominant grape variety (e.g., Pinot Noir, Chardonnay, Sauvignon Blanc). Often credited with having coined the term VARIETAL, though some believe the word was invented by his former deputy ALEXIS LICHINE.

Show. Snob term used in verb form to indicate how a wine, usually of a noteworthy older vintage, is expressing itself at the moment of its evaluation—usually in relation to its "performance" at an earlier tasting. *Call me nuts, but the '83s are* showing *better than the '82s.*

Site-expressive. Sharpened adjectival evocation of *TERROIR,* referring not just to the area where a wine's grapes are grown, but to the unmistakable influence of a specific vineyard site on a wine's character—be it a stony flavor from the soil, elevated ACIDITY as a result of altitude, or some other flavor sensation(s) driven not by the meddling winemaker but by the unduplicable quirks of a certain patch of earth. *This* site-expressive *wine fairly tingles with the minerality that defines Les Clos.*

Spoofalated. Scornful term invented by old-line wine-makers to describe any wine so bombastic and over-manipulated by man—usually via excessive oak usage, but sometimes by way of overripeness or MICRO-OXYGENATION—that it lacks any discernible VA-RIETAL character. *I couldn't bring myself to tell Dad that the Chilean wine he so proudly gets by the case from Costco is a ghastly, overbearing,* spoofalated *grape beverage.*

Stelvin closure. Dorky handle for a kind of sophisti-cated screwcap developed specifically for wine bottles in the 1970s, and taken up as a cause in recent years by NEW WORLD winemakers, especially in Australia and New Zealand. Though traditionalists relish and fetishize the ritual of extracting a cork from a wine bot-tle (their feelings stoked by a powerful cork lobby), many Progressivist Snobs are getting past the screw-cap's déclassé associations and adopting the Stelvin. *We more than made up for the margin we lost to cork taint by putting together an all-*Stelvin *list at our bistro.*

Stemmy. Pejorative term for a wine made from grapes that were left too long in contact with their stems dur-ing the fermentation process, resulting in a bitter fla-vor. *Odd, geranium-like nose, metallic and* stemmy *on the palate, dusty finish. Abysmal.*

Stickie. Snob nickname for sweet wines such as Sauternes, ostensibly derived from the fact that their sugar-rich drippings are sticky to the touch. Generally credited as a coinage, as most loony wine slang is, to the Australians. *We ended the night with a killer* stickie *from Hungary.*

Stone, Larry. Hyperpalated wine prodigy turned bow-tied MASTER SOMMELIER, widely considered to be the foremost in his field in the United States. One of a mere handful of serious-minded young cork-pullers when he first attacted national attention in the late 1980s at Charlie Trotter's in Chicago, Stone hit his stride in the early 1990s at San Francisco's Rubicon, a restaurant expressly conceived by its owner, Drew Nieporent, as a wine mecca and showcase for Stone's talents. The avatar of the new-breed, customer-friendly, adorably compact American sommelier, Stone managed to bridge the gap between

Larry Stone

Snobs and normal wine enthusiasts, so enjoying the everyday grind of patrolling the floor that he remained at it longer than most, only recently hanging up his TASTEVIN to become general manager of Francis Coppola's Rubicon estate in Napa.

Straw-colored. Default lyrical descriptor for white wines, used to evoke the pastoral aspects of viticulture and obscure the fact that most white wines resemble urine or cooking oil.

Structure. Grandiose architectural term for a wine's overall body and MOUTHFEEL. A tart, high-acid wine is considered "firm" in structure, and a tannic wine more "powerful" or TIGHT, while a softer, super-ripe style might be saddled with a deadly structural pejorative such as FLABBY. *I really don't know what all the fuss is about with these Oregon Pinots, 'cause most of them lack any classical* structure.

Suckling, James. Middle-aged leisure journalist and European Bureau Chief for the *Wine Spectator,* known for catering to a wealthy, Centurion Card–holding readership. Fond of Cuban cigars and the attendant perks of his beat (luxury-resort stays, part-time residency in Italy, backstage Stones passes, the company of Marvin Shanken), Suckling, who apprenticed under ALEXIS LICHINE, is not shy in projecting his sense of authority in his wine reviews, which often read like coronations. Like ROBERT PARKER, he is a polarizer of Snobs, some of whom value his expertise and experience, others of whom find him an insufferable tool of the fractional-jet-share set.

Super-Seconds. Nickname for the better châteaux among the *deuxièmes* CRUs, or Second Growths, of Bordeaux. To appreciate the consistent excellence of a Léoville–Las Cases or a Cos d'Estournel is to laugh in the faces of the label whores who only buy First Growths; and to know which Seconds outperformed Firsts in a given vintage is to wade deeply into bona-fide Snobbery.

Super Tuscan. Snob moniker for a superior class of unclassified red wine from Tuscany. Legend has it that a British writer coined the phrase in the '60s after tasting SASSICAIA, a wine that, like its Super Tuscan brethren, was bafflingly labeled a *vino de tavola*—a humble table wine—despite its obvious world-class quality. Still, it wasn't until the 1990s that Super Tuscans registered with Snobs, who before then hewed to the conventional wisdom that only such government-delimited appellations of origin as Chianti Classico could demarcate a first-rate Italian wine. That Super Tuscans have since skyrocketed into the high three digits in price is testament not only to Snob frenzy, but to the supreme power of branding, even if the brand has a tongue-twisting name like Ornellaia or Tignanello.

Sutcliffe, Serena, and David Peppercorn. British Wine Snob supercouple, she the head of Sotheby's international wine department, he a venerable authority on Bordeaux. A sassy, luxuriantly white-maned presence, Sutcliffe inspires crushes in the male-dominated wine world much as JANCIS ROBINSON does, while the much-older Peppercorn is esteemed as "the quiet one" among Britain's oeno-elders, neither as populist as HUGH JOHNSON nor as plummy as MICHAEL BROADBENT.

Tanky. Dismissive term for a stale wine that was stored too long in a large vessel rather than bottled in timely fashion. *Oh, that Zin is just flat and* tanky; *I don't know where they get off charging $45 for it.*

Tannin. Naturally occurring chemical compound found in the stems, seeds, and skin of grapes, as well as in the wooden casks in which many wines are aged. Especially prominent in red-wine grapes like Nebbiolo and Syrah, tannins are both derided by Snobs for the unwelcome, bitter-tea astringency they lend to young or poorly made wines and embraced for their role as a natural preservative and antioxidant in slow-developing wines that must be cellared for years, if not decades. *Gagged on the '01 at the barrel tasting in Sonoma a few years ago, but now its* tannins *are nicely integrated with luscious cassis and dark-fruit flavors, and an awesome espresso finish.*

Tastevin. Silver wine-tasting cup, usually hung from a chain and worn around the neck of a tuxedoed sommelier still living in the year 1962. Though largely relegated to the dustbin of wine history, the tastevin is significant to Snobs as

Tastevin

a test of erudition, since a true Snob knows it was originally designed for use in winery cellars, not restaurants; the silver material and dimples in the bottom cause light to reflect through the wine and help the vintner assess clarity.

Tasting notes. Traditionally, the jottings of collectors and enthusiasts about the wines they've drunk, kept for reference and memory-jogging purposes, usually in picturesquely frayed notebooks. More recently, a marketing ploy by winemakers themselves, who preempt any sense of discovery by offering cheat-sheet notes on a bottle's back label. *Grapes: 100% Pinot Noir.* Tasting notes: *Aromas of blackberry and butterscotch, with black cherry on the palate and a licorice finish.*

Tanzer, Stephen. Prolific publisher-writer of low-key wine newsletter (officially known as the *International Wine Cellar*) that, since its inception in 1985, has positioned itself as the more thoughtful, more writerly, less hypey alternative to ROBERT PARKER's *Wine Advocate* —though even Parker rates it highly (albeit without assigning it a numerical score). Tanzer provides an authoritative voice for wineries and wine stores searching for quotes to use in advertising, especially when no such quotes already exist from Parker or the *Wine Spectator.*

TBA. Abbreviation for Trockenbeerenauslese, the high-priced, long-aging German dessert wine as beloved by Snobs for its unwieldy name (pronounced truck-en-BEAR-en-nowse-LAY-zuh) as for its honeyed color and flavor. Even more complex than an Auslese or a Beerenauslese, late-harvest wines made from overripe white grapes infected with the fungus BOTRYTIS, TBA is made from shriveled grapes individually selected by the grower, thus making the wine inherently small-batch and Snob-treasured in nature.

Tchelistcheff, André. Russian-born, Toulouse-Lautrec–sized oenologist (1901–1994) and leading light of the ascendant Napa Valley of the post-Prohibition era. Summoned to California from his adopted France in 1938 by Georges de Latour, the French owner of Beaulieu Vineyards in Rutherford, Tchelistcheff used his expertise to cultivate the state's first superior Cabernet Sauvignons, and remained with the winemaker for some forty years. For all his loyalty to Beaulieu, Tchelistcheff also blazed a trail for today's FLYING WINEMAKERS, having started a sideline as a handsomely compensated consultant when MICHEL ROLLAND was still suckling at the teat in Libourne.

Terroir. Unimpeachable cornerstone of the Classicist Snob's vocabulary, denoting the "total natural environment" of the grapevine—the climate in which it's grown, the chemical and mineral composition of the soil from which it's sprouted, the animals that poop near it, etc. Only the most wizened and Francophilic of Snobs can carry off the phrase *goût de terroir* (taste of *terroir*), usually while praising a cellared, old-growth French wine at the expense of some drink-now FRUIT BOMB bottled by a GARAGISTE.

Tertiary. Shorthand for *tertiary aromas,* one of the many quasi-scientific tasting terms bequeathed by EMILE PEYNAUD, and referring to the beguiling bouquets unique to aged wines. Whereas "primary" aromas are defined as the straightforward, fruity smells derived from grapes, and the more vinous "secondary" aromas derive from the fermentation process, "tertiary" smells—your dried flowers, your PIE SPICES, and all the sundry ethereal scents that lend a wine COMPLEXITY—arrive only with patience and time. *Now, with more than a decade of bottle age on it, the '96 Cos d'Estournel is starting to give off more clove, florals, and other sexy* tertiaries *on the nose.*

Theise, Terry. Impish, bearded importer whose gonzo advocacy on behalf of Austrian and German wineries has endeared him to the intellectual, non-humidor-owning wing of Wine Snobbery. Married to the noted chef Odessa Piper, and often referred to simply as Theise (much as the Canadian alt-popstress Leslie Feist goes simply by Feist), he has won wine-world fame as the chief American champion of unusual, small-production wines that induce rhapsodic delight in otherwise jaded sommeliers, e.g., German Rieslings, Austrian Grüners, and GROWER CHAMPAGNES. Theise acolytes devotedly devour the catalogs he churns out for the importer-distributor Michael Skurnik Wines, written in a dense, loopy, Thoreau–meets–Dr. Bronner style and often preceded with a "Theise Manifesto" that includes the sentiment "Lots of wines, many of them good wines, let you taste the noise. But only the best let you taste the silence."

Terry Theise

Throw. Verb used anthropomorphically to underscore that wine is *alive* and, less lyrically, to describe how aged wines deposit sediment in bottles. In Snob parlance, a wine does not "have" sediment, or even "leave" sediment, but rather *throws* sediment—casting off its youthful, tannic cloak in its march toward maturity. *Make sure you stand up that Giacosa a good hour before you decant it, because it's throwing a lot of fine sediment right now.*

Tight. Adjective used to describe young, virginal wines whose flavors and aromas seem muted on account of their undeveloped TANNINS; derived, probably, from the astringent, puckery sensation such wines impart. *The '96 remains tight, that luscious redberry fruit still hidden behind a brick wall of tannin. Give it another four or five years.*

Turley, Helen. Astonishingly high-priced California winemaking consultant who has crafted several of California's astonishingly high-priced wines, such as ANN COLGIN's; the American analog to MICHEL ROLLAND. Working with her viticulturist husband, John Wetlaufer, Turley assumes control of every aspect of the grape-growing and winemaking processes, and takes a cut of her employer's profits—an audacious approach that appalls Euro-purists, who also lament Turley's technique-over-*TERROIR* philosophy, but delights wealthy Napa arrivistes looking to purchase instant PARKER credibility.

Helen Turley

WHICH TYPE OF WINE
SNOB ARE YOU?

A Spotter's Guide

1. THE TITAN

THUMBNAIL: Financier with six homes, the largest of which has a cellar that holds 5,000-plus bottles and is more habitable than most normal people's above-ground dwellings

FAVORITE WINES: The blue chips, e.g., First-Growth Bordeaux, Grand Cru Burgundy, Barolo, and Super Tuscans

PLUMAGE AND MARKINGS: Perma-tan; nimbus of gray-to-white hair; New Millennium Wall Street–casual getup of tailored shirt, cuffed khakis, and bespoke loafers with no socks

QUOTE: "I'm a seller on this '82 Lafite. Maybe it's a bad bottle. Hell, let's open another one!"

2. THE SOMMELIER

THUMBNAIL: Wiry, short dandy with eccentric but tidy facial hair; volatile and bipolar

FAVORITE WINES: "Food-friendly" and as obscure as possible, e.g., Austrian Grüner Veltliner, German Riesling, Italian Lagrein

PLUMAGE AND MARKINGS: Dark, double-vented, slim-cut Euro-suit; bold tie with absurdly large Windsor knot; flashy socks; architectural eyewear

QUOTE: "Look, I can sell you some spoofalated stuff from my list—I *can* do that—but Chef's food demands something with acidity and balance. Let me take care of you."

3. THE SCHLUMP

THUMBNAIL: Wine journalist or small-scale importer; rumpled, righteous, and forever determined to defend "real wine" against the barbaric hordes of Robert Parker acolytes

FAVORITE WINES: Not unlike those of the Sommelier, but cheaper, and often from supposedly "off" vintages that the Sommelier failed to "get"

PLUMAGE AND MARKINGS: Merrell slip-ons; messenger bag; tweed blazer overlaid with fleece parka; dandruff

QUOTE: "Harmony is more important than intensity! Oh, and can we share a cab?"

4. THE ARRIVISTE

THUMBNAIL: Driven, still-youngish professional with wine acumen borne of an expense account and several years of staying in Ritz-Carltons; theatrically bossy and inquisitive with service providers

FAVORITE WINES: Kistler Chardonnay, Justin Isosceles and other Meritages, Brunello di Montalcino, Australian Shiraz (but just for "around the house")

PLUMAGE AND MARKINGS: Copious hair product; expensive but off-the-rack suits from luxury clothiers

QUOTE: "Caitlin and I fell in love with Brunello at our wedding in Tuscany."

5. THE ENGLISHMAN

THUMBNAIL: Quavery, snaggle-toothed senior citizen with forelock forever tumbling forward

FAVORITE WINES: "A nice Claret" (aka Bordeaux) and anything else noble, old, and French

PLUMAGE AND MARKINGS: Slender, feminine hands with tapered fingers; "a suit of clothes from Huntsman," often with waistcoat; trilby or other suitably retro headwear

QUOTE: "Madam, I don't mean to be dogmatic, but one should never wear a scent to a wine tasting."

UC-Davis. Branch of the University of California that, since shortly after the repeal of Prohibition, has been the home of the foremost American academic institution devoted to the making and study of wine, the Department of Viticulture and Enology (V&E in Snob shorthand). Long derided by Snobs, especially of the *TERROIR*-ist variety, for promulgating a scientific, machine-age, high-yield approach to winemaking that resulted in the California jug-wine boom of the midcentury, UC-Davis has recently become a Snob-admired haven for wonky progressivists such as the professor who created the WINE AROMA WHEEL. As such, the V&E department is now handsomely endowed by the MONDAVI family, the *Wine Spectator,* and other major wine players.

Unfiltered. Adjective describing wine that has been minimally subjected or unsubjected to any filtering to remove solid particles. While this practice is distressingly common among neophyte winemakers hoping to concoct huge, vulgar FRUIT BOMBS, it is also favored by minimal-interventionist purists and tradesmen like KERMIT LYNCH, who believe that not filtering produces a raw, tongue-stainingly authentic

JUICE that's exuberantly colored and CONCEN-TRATED.

Ungrafted. Deeply romanticized term for a vine or vineyard area, specifically one in the OLD WORLD, that was spared from the ravages of PHYLLOXERA. Whereas the majority of European vineyards had to be replanted in the late nineteenth century using American rootstocks that had developed an immunity to the pest, certain stands of vines—due to their remoteness, the composition of their soils, or plain dumb luck—managed to avoid phylloxera infestation. Such vines—pockets of which are found in Spain, Sicily, France, and elsewhere—are Snob-prized not just for their uniqueness and cachet but for the fact that they are perceived as unviolated, unadulterated signposts of primordial *TERROIR*.

THE WINE SNOB CHEAT SHEET FOR CONFUSING SIMILARITIES

Stag's Leap Wine Cellars is the Napa Valley winery established in 1972 by Warren Winiarski. **Stags' Leap Winery** is the Napa Valley winery that was established in 1893, revived in the 1970s by Carl Doumani, and subsequently purchased by Beringer Wine Estates.

Krug is the venerable French Champagne house now owned by luxury-brand conglomerate LVMH. **Charles Krug** is the venerable Napa winery owned by the Peter Mondavi wing of the Mondavi family.

The Wine Advocate is the bare-bones, ad-free bimonthly periodical put out by Robert Parker, known for the numerical scores it assigns wines. *The Wine Spectator* is the glossy, ad-heavy, sixteen-times-a-year periodical put out by Marvin Shanken, known for its luxe-lifestyle articles and ubiquity in business-class airport lounges.

Vino Nobile di Montepulciano is the local wine of the Tuscan town of Montepulciano, made from Sangiovese grapes. **Montepulciano d'Abruzzo** is a wine made in the central Italian region of Abruzzo from Montepulciano grapes, which are native to the southern part of the country.

Barbaresco is a noble Italian red wine made from Nebbiolo grapes. **Barbera** is a kind of red-wine grape used in Italian wines less posh than Barbaresco and in cheap blends overseas.

Muscadet is a dry Loire Valley white wine made from Melon de Bourgogne grapes. **Muscat** is a kind of grape grown in several varieties in several countries, usually for the purpose of making dessert wines.

Pouilly Fumé is a difficult-to-pronounce appellation in the Loire Valley, near Sancerre, that offers crisp and grassy white wines made from

Sauvignon Blanc grapes. **Pouilly Fuissé** is a difficult-to-pronounce part of the Mâcon region of Burgundy that offers a rich white wine made from Chardonnay grapes.

Varietal. Fancy term for "wine made primarily or entirely from one kind of grape." Until the 1970s, wines were generally ID'd with low-rent, jug-worthy descriptors (e.g., "hearty Burgundy," "white table wine") or with a prestigious geographical appellation (e.g., Bordeaux, Sancerre, Saint-Émilion). But as California began to assert itself as a wine region in the 1970s, NEW WORLD winemakers discovered that marketing their wines by grape name (e.g., Pinot Noir, Zinfandel, Cabernet Sauvignon) proved seductive to prestige-minded buyers. Varietal labeling has since spread to Europe, especially Italy, whose winemakers have found a robust market for Yankee friendly wines made from (and named for) Nebbiolo, Sangiovese, and Aglianico grapes.

Vertical. Snob shorthand for *vertical tasting,* a tasting (or menu listing) in which a series of vintages of a single wine is presented chronologically, typically from oldest to youngest. Given that a "taste memory" of a wine's diverse vintages is a Snob mark of distinction, taking part in a vertical, whether through deep-pocketed exploration of a GRAND AWARD restaurant's list or through the generosity of a winemaker or a private collector, is crucial to a fledgling Snob's social development.

Vigneron. French term for "winemaker," used by Anglophone wine writers and diarists to suggest hale-fellow-well-met bonhomie, much in the way one would call a bartender a "barkeep." *"Salut!" shouted the* vigneron, *a stout, ruddy gent whose steel-rimmed spectacles suggested a fierce intellectualism beneath the rustic façade.*

Vine density. Viticultural term bandied about by Snobs in order to establish their production-method bona fides. Until the 1980s, American winemakers favored wide spacings between individual vines—roughly eight feet apart, with twelve feet between rows—which led to high grape yields and affordable wines. More recently, aspirational American growers have aped the traditional French model of one meter–by–one meter spacings, which results in far fewer grapes but wines of greater depth, COMPLEXITY, and expense. *It was after sampling the first bottling of Opus One that I realized how serious Mondavi was about* vine density.

Volatile acidity. Common wine defect caused by excess production of acetic acid, resulting in a vinegary smell. Traditionally abbreviated to V.A. by Snobs, who like to use the term to intimidate pourers and sommeliers. *I'm getting a lot of* V.A. *on this—get this crap outta my face!*

Wine Aroma Wheel. Hyperprecise yet fanciful wine-understanding tool developed in 1990 by UC-DAVIS professor Ann Noble. Resembling a baroque version of the spinner that comes with the game Twister, the wheel's descriptors—grouped in terms of theme by color-coded wedges (e.g., purple for "Fruity," green for "Earthy," red for "Microbiological") and in terms of specificity by concentric circles (the most general in the inner tier, the most specific in the outer tier)—enable even novice Snobs to unleash intimidatingly analytical wine-talk with ease. Among the wheel's more outré (and therefore Snob-impressing) descriptors are "Wet Dog," "Sweaty," and "Plastic."

Wine Aroma Wheel

Wine club. Subscription-style membership program in which a customer pays a vintner (or, occasionally, a winemaker) a large fee in exchange for a monthly delivery of carefully selected wines and, usually, the expert's pertinent TASTING NOTES. Less egregiously show-offy than engaging a store's CELLAR MANAGEMENT services, belonging to a wine club allows a fledgling Snob to broaden his horizons without actually entering a shop and publicly revealing his knowledge gaps. *I didn't know squat about Gewürz until my man Rob hooked me up some good Boxler shit through his VIP* wine club.

Wine director. Glorified term for "sommelier," usually assigned as a sop to a harried head man at a restaurant that keeps a large cellar and prides itself on wine service, but whose ownership is more generous with titles than with wages. In the current age of "hospitality groups," a wine director sometimes oversees the lists and cellars of several restaurants, with their respective sommeliers reporting to him. Also sometimes known, rather office-park-ishly, as a *beverage director.*

Winiarski, Warren. Rumpled, professorial, Chicago-born founder of Napa Valley's Stag's Leap Wine Cellars, whose very first vintage of Cabernet Sauvignon, the '73, triumphed at the fabled JUDGMENT OF PARIS. Oft mentioned in the same breath as JOE HEITZ and ROBERT MONDAVI, Winiarski is Snob-adored for his brown-dirt, tractor-straddlin' authenticity, and for being the Napa pioneer who most resembles an actual farmer.

Zero manipulation. Righteous buzz-term increasingly in Snob circulation as the backlash grows against consultant-goosed wines that are less about *TERROIR* than about the winemaker's ego and such advanced techniques as MICRO-OXYGENATION. Sonoma County's Peterson Winery has gone so far as to formally name its inexpensive red table wine Zero Manipulation, the first bottling of which was billed as "a good, honest wine produced in the style practiced by the Italian immigrants who originally settled the Dry Creek Valley."

Zraly, Kevin. Bearded, gregarious sommelier emeritus, unusually unrunty for his profession, who made his name as a twentysomething wine prodigy at Windows on the World when it opened in 1976, and who has gone on to become America's foremost wine educator. While no Snob would ever cop to having attended Zraly's beginner-friendly Windows on the World Wine School—which has soldiered on in Midtown Manhattan since 9/11—he retains high Snob cred for the massive, American-heavy list he put together for Windows, and for his recent activity as a blogger on ROBERT PARKER's Web site. *If anyone can come up with a Cal red to pair with tilapia, it's* Zraly.

About the Authors

DAVID KAMP has been a writer and editor for *Vanity Fair* and *GQ* magazines for over a decade and began his career at *Spy* magazine. He lives in New York City.

DAVID LYNCH is a James Beard Award–winning writer and sommelier. He is a contributor to magazines such as *GQ* and *Food & Wine*, the author of *Vino Italiano: The Regional Wines of Italy*, and the former wine director of New York's famed Babbo Ristorante.

About the Illustrator

ROSS MACDONALD's illustrations have appeared in many publications from *The New Yorker* and *Vanity Fair* to *Rolling Stone* and the *Wall Street Journal*. Two of his children's books, *Another Perfect Day* and *Achoo! Bang! Crash! The Noisy Alphabet*, have won *Publishers Weekly*'s Best Books of the Year awards for their categories. MacDonald lives in Connecticut with his wife, two children, four cats, two dogs, and a large collection of nineteenth-century type and printing equipment.